Color Schemes For The Flower Garden

Gertrude Jekyll

COLOUR SCHEMES FOR THE FLOWER GARDEN

BY

GERTRUDE JEKYLL

FOURTH EDITION

LONDON:

PUBLISHED AT THE OFFICES OF "COUNTRY LIFE," Ltd.
20, TAVISTOCK STREET, COVENT GARDEN, W.C., AND BY
GEORGE NEWNES, Ltd., 8—11, SOUTHAMPTON STREET
STRAND, W.C. NEW YORK : CHARLES SCRIBNER'S SONS
1919

Gordens

WHITE ROSE AND LAVENDER.

PREFACE

THE continued demand for this book has necessitated the preparation of a fourth edition. The author has been much gratified by the many letters that have been received from unknown correspondents expressing grateful acknowledgment of its helpfulness, and for the encouragement and inspiration they have derived from its pages.

G. J.

INTRODUCTION

To plant and maintain a flower border, *with a good scheme for colour*, is by no means the easy thing that is commonly supposed.

I believe that the only way in which it can be made successful is to devote certain borders to certain times of year ; each border or garden region to be bright for from one to three months.

Nothing seems to me more unsatisfactory than the border that in spring shows a few patches of flowering bulbs in ground otherwise looking empty, or with tufts of herbaceous plants just coming through. Then the bulbs die down, and their place is wanted for something that comes later. Either the ground will then show bare patches, or the place of the bulbs will be forgotten and they will be cruelly stabbed by fork or trowel when it is wished to put something in the apparently empty space.

For many years I have been working at these problems in my own garden, and, having come to certain conclusions, can venture to put them forth with some confidence. I may mention that from the nature of the ground, in its original state partly wooded and partly bare field, and from its having been brought into cultivation and some sort of shape before it was known where the house now upon it would exactly stand, the garden has less general unity of design than I should have wished. The position and general form of its various portions were accepted mainly according to their natural conditions, so that the garden ground, though but of small extent, falls into different regions, with a general, but not altogether definite, cohesion.

I am strongly of opinion that the possession of a quantity of plants, however good the plants may be themselves and however ample their number, does not make a garden ; it only makes a *collection*. Having got the plants, the great thing is to use them with careful selection and definite intention. Merely having them, or having them planted unassorted in garden spaces, is only like having a box of paints from the best colourman, or, to go one step further, it is like having portions of these paints set out upon a palette. This does not constitute a picture ; and it seems to me that the duty we owe to our gardens and to our own bettering in our gardens is so to use the plants that they shall form beautiful pictures ; and that, while delighting our eyes, they should be always training those eyes to a more exalted criticism ; to a state of mind and artistic conscience that will not tolerate bad or careless combination or any sort of misuse of plants, but in which it becomes a point of honour to be always striving for the best.

It is just in the way it is done that lies the whole difference between commonplace gardening and gardening that may rightly claim to rank as a fine art.

Given the same space of ground and the same material, they may either be fashioned into a dream of beauty, a place of perfect rest and refreshment of mind and body—a series of soul-satisfying pictures—a treasure of well-set jewels ; or they may be so misused that everything is jarring and displeasing. To learn how to perceive the difference and how to do right is to apprehend gardening as a fine art. In practice it is to place every plant or group of plants with such thoughtful care and definite intention that they shall form a part of a harmonious whole, and that successive portions, or in some cases even single details, shall show a series of pictures. It is so to regulate the trees and undergrowth of the wood that their lines and masses come into beautiful form and harmonious proportion ; it is to be always watching, noting and doing, and putting oneself meanwhile into closest acquaintance and sympathy with the growing things.

In this spirit, the garden and woodland, such as they are, have been formed. There have been many failures, but, every now and then, I am encouraged and rewarded by a certain measure of success. Yet, as the critical faculty becomes keener, so does the standard of aim rise higher ; and, year by year, the desired point seems always to elude attainment.

But, as I may perhaps have taken more trouble in working out certain problems, and given more thought to methods of arranging growing flowers, especially in ways of colour-combination, than amateurs in general, I have thought that it may be helpful to some of them to describe as well as I can by word, and to show by plan and picture, what I have tried to do, and to point out where I have succeeded and where I have failed.

I must ask my kind readers not to take it amiss if I mention here that I cannot undertake to show it them on the spot. I am a solitary worker; I am growing old and tired, and suffer from very bad and painful sight. My garden is my workshop, my private study and place of rest. For the sake of health and reasonable enjoyment of life it is necessary to keep it quite private, and to refuse the many applications of those who offer it visits. My oldest friends can now only be admitted. So I ask my readers to spare me the painful task of writing long letters of excuse and explanation; a task that has come upon me almost daily of late years in the summer months, that has sorely tried my weak and painful eyes, and has added much to the difficulty of getting through an already over-large correspondence.

CONTENTS

CONTENTS

LIST OF ILLUSTRATIONS

LIST OF ILLUSTRATIONS

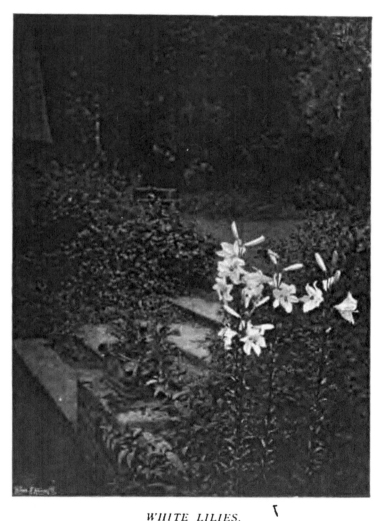

WHITE LILIES.

COLOUR SCHEMES FOR THE FLOWER GARDEN

CHAPTER I

A MARCH STUDY AND THE BORDER OF EARLY BULBS

THERE comes a day towards the end of March when there is but little wind, and that is from the west or even south-west. The sun has gained much power, so that it is pleasant to sit out in the garden, or, better still, in some sunny nook of sheltered woodland. There is such a place among silver-trunked Birches, with here and there the splendid richness of masses of dark Holly. The rest of the background above eye-level is of the warm bud-colour of the summer-leafing trees, and, below, the fading rust of the now nearly flattened fronds of last year's Bracken, and the still paler drifts of leaves from neighbouring Oaks and Chestnuts. The sunlight strikes brightly on the silver stems of the Birches, and casts their shadows clear-cut across the grassy woodland ride. The grass is barely green as yet, but has the faint winter green of herbage not yet grown and still powdered with the short remnants of the fine-leaved, last-year-mown heath grasses.

Brown leaves still hang on young Beech and Oak. The trunks of the Spanish Chestnuts are elephant-grey, a notable contrast to the sudden, vivid shafts of the Birches. Some groups of the pale early Pyrenean Daffodil gleam level on the ground a little way forward.

It is the year's first complete picture of flower-effect in the woodland landscape. The place is not very far from the house, within the nearest hundred yards of the copse, where flowers seem to be more in place than further away. Looking to the left, the long ridge and south slope of the house-roof is seen through the leafless trees, though the main wall-block is hidden by the sheltering Hollies and Junipers.

Coming down towards the garden by another broad grassy way, that goes westward through the Chestnuts and then turns towards the down-hill north, there comes yet another deviation through Rhododendrons and Birches to the main lawn. But before the last turn there is a pleasant mass of colour showing in the wood-edge on the dead-leaf carpet. It is a straggling group of *Daphne Mezereum*, with some clumps of red Lent Hellebores, and, to the front, some half-connected patches of the common Dog-tooth Violet. The nearly related combination of colour is a delight to the trained colour-eye. There is nothing brilliant; it is all restrained—refined; in harmony with the veiled light that reaches the flowers through the great clumps of Hollies and tall half-overhead Chestnuts and neighbouring Beech. The colours are all a little "sad," as the old writers so aptly say of the flower-tints of secondary strength. But it is a perfect picture. One comes to it again and again as one does to any picture that is good to live with.

To devise these living pictures from simple well-known flowers seems to me the best thing to do in gardening. Whether it is the putting together of two or three kinds of plants, or even of one kind only in some happy setting, or whether it is the ordering of a much larger number of plants, as in a flower-border of middle and late summer, the intention is always the same. Whether the arrangement is simple and modest, whether it is bold and gorgeous, whether it is obvious or whether it is subtle, the aim is always to use the plants to the best of one's means and intelligence so as to form pictures of living beauty.

It is a thing that I see so rarely attempted, and that seems to me so important, that the wish to suggest it to others, and to give an idea of examples that I have worked out, in however modest a way, is the purpose of this book.

These early examples within the days of March are of special interest because as yet flowers are but few ; the mind is less distracted by much variety than later in the year, and is more readily concentrated on the few things that may be done and observed ; so that the necessary restriction is a good preparation, by easy steps, for the wider field of observation that is presented later.

Now we pass on through the dark masses of Rhododendron and the Birches that shoot up among them. How the silver stems, blotched and banded with varied browns and greys so deep in tone that they show like a luminous black, tell among the glossy Rhododendron green ; and how strangely different is the way of growth of the two kinds of tree ; the tall white trunks spearing up through the dense, dark, leathery leaf-masses of solid, roundish outline, with their delicate network of reddish branch and spray gently swaying far overhead !

Now we come to the lawn, which slopes a little downward to the north. On the right it has a low retaining-wall, whose top line is level ; it bears up a border and pathway next the house's western face. The border and wall are all of a piece, for it is a dry wall partly planted with the same shrubby and half-shrubby things that are in the earth above. They have been comforting to look at all the winter ; a pleasant grey coating of Phlomis, Lavender, Rosemary, Cistus, and Santolina ; and at the end and angle where the wall is highest, a mass of *Pyrus japonica*, planted both above and below, already showing its rose-red bloom. At one point at the foot of the wall is a strong tuft of *Iris stylosa* whose first blooms appeared in November. This capital plant flowers bravely all through the winter in any intervals of open weather. It likes a sunny place against a wall in poor soil. If it is planted in better ground the leaves grow very tall and it gives but little bloom.

Now we pass among some shrub-clumps, and at the end come upon a cheering sight ; a tree of *Magnolia conspicua* bearing hundreds of its great white cups of fragrant bloom. Just before reaching it, and taking part with it in the garden picture, are some tall bushes

IRIS STYLOSA.

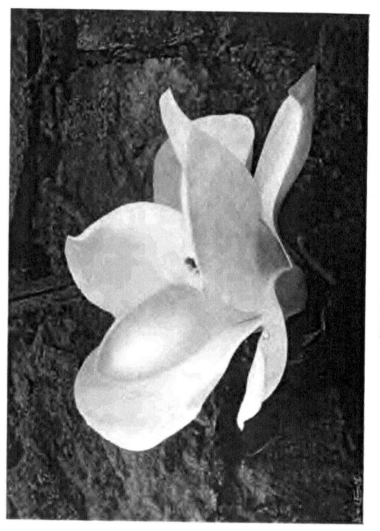

MAGNOLIA CONSPICUA.

of *Forsythia suspensa*, tossing out many-feet-long branches loaded with their burden of clear yellow flowers. They are ten to twelve feet high, and one looks up at much of the bloom clear-cut against the pure blue of the sky ; the upper part of the Magnolia also shows against the sky. Here there is a third flower-picture ; this time of warm white and finest yellow on brilliant blue, and out in open sunlight. Among the Forsythias is also a large bush of *Magnolia stellata*, whose milk-white flowers may be counted by the thousand. As the earlier *M. conspicua* goes out of bloom it comes into full bearing, keeping pace with the Forsythia, whose season runs on well into April.

It is always a little difficult to find suitable places for the early bulbs. Many of them can be enjoyed in rough and grassy places, but we also want to combine them into pretty living pictures in the garden proper.

Nothing seems to me more unsatisfactory than the usual way of having them scattered about in small patches in the edges of flower-borders, where they only show as little disconnected dabs of colour, and where they are necessarily in danger of disturbance and probable injury when their foliage has died down and their places are wanted for summer flowers.

It was a puzzle for many years to know how to treat these early bulbs, but at last a plan was devised that seems so satisfactory that I have no hesitation in advising it for general adoption.

On the further side of a path that bounds my June garden is a border about seventy feet long and ten feet wide. At every ten feet along the back is a

larch post planted with a free-growing Rose. These
are not only to clothe their posts, but to grow into
garlands swinging on slack chains from post to post.
Beyond are Bamboos, and then an old hedge-bank
with Scotch Firs, Oaks, Thorns, &c. The border
slopes upwards from the path, forming a bank of
gentle ascent. It was first planted with hardy Ferns
in bold drifts ; Male Fern for the most part, because
it is not only handsome but extremely persistent,
the fronds remaining green into the winter. The Fern-
spaces are shown in the plan by diagonal hatching ;
between them come the bulbs, with a general edging
to the front of mossy Saxifrage.

The colour scheme begins with the pink of *Megasea
ligulata*, and with the lower-toned pinks of *Fumaria
bulbosa* and the Dog-tooth Violets (*Erythronium*). At
the back of these are Lent Hellebores of dull red colouring, agreeing charmingly with the colour of the bulbs.
A few white Lent Hellebores are at the end ; they
have turned to greenish white by the time the rather
late *Scilla amœna* is in bloom. Then comes a brilliant
patch of pure blue with white—*Scilla sibirica* and
white Hyacinths, followed by the also pure blues of
Scilla bifolia and *Chionodoxa* and the later, more purple
blue of Grape Hyacinth. A long drift of white Crocus
comes next, in beauty in the border's earliest days ;
and later, the blue-white of *Puschkinia ;* then again
pure blue and white of *Chionodoxa* and white Hyacinth.

Now the colours change to white and yellow and
golden foliage, with the pretty little pale trumpet
Daffodil Consul Crawford, and beyond it the stronger

MAGNOLIA STELLATA.

FERNS IN THE BULB BORDER.

yellow of two other small early kinds—*N. nanus* and the charming little *N. minor*, quite distinct though so often confounded with *nanus* in gardens. With these, and in other strips and patches towards the end of the border, are plantings of the Golden Valerian, so useful for its bright yellow foliage quite early in the year. The leaves of the Orange Day-lily are also of a pale yellowish-green colour when they first come up, and are used at the end of the border. These plants of golden and pale foliage are also placed in a further region beyond the plan, and show to great advantage as the eye enfilades the border and reaches the more distant places. Before the end of the bulb-border is reached there is once more a drift of harmonised faint pink colouring of *Megasea* and the little *Fumaria*, (also known as *Corydalis bulbosa*) with the pale early Pyrenean Daffodil, *N. pallidus præcox*.

The bulb-flowers are not all in bloom exactly at the same time, but there is enough of the colour intended to give the right effect in each grouping. Standing at the end, just beyond the Dog-tooth Violets, the arrangement and progression of colour is pleasant and interesting, and in some portions vivid ; the pure blues in the middle spaces being much enhanced by the yellow flowers and golden foliage that follow.

A nearly similar arrangement of flowers for earliest spring has been made at a place where a path from the lawn branches into three grassy ways up into the copse. The planted promontory is a bank rising from the grass paths and is set with a few large stones. As it is backed by Hollies and Junipers, and then by the Birches of the wood, it has a back planting of such shrubs as both accord in colour with the flowering plants and lead suitably to the further woodland. These are *Rhododendron præcox* and *Andromeda* (*Pieris*) *floribunda*—a wide-spreading Savin is already behind them—while the front planting is stiffened by some of the early blooming Heaths, *Erica carnea* in one or two colourings and *E. hybrida.* There is also, though the bloom will not be till later, a kind of backbone of Alpenrose (*Rhododendron ferruginium*), which gives a certain aspect of strength and solidity.

Through April and May the leaves of the bulbs are growing tall, and their seed-pods are carefully removed to prevent exhaustion. By the end of May the Ferns are throwing up their leafy crooks ; by June the feathery fronds are displayed in all their tender freshness ; they spread over the whole bank, and we forget that there are any bulbs between. By the time the June garden, whose western boundary it forms, has come into fullest bloom it has become a completely furnished bank of Fern-beauty.

CHAPTER II

THE WOOD

TEN acres is but a small area for a bit of woodland, yet it can be made apparently much larger by well-considered treatment. As the years pass and the different portions answer to careful guidance, I am myself surprised to see the number and wonderful variety of the pictures of sylvan beauty that it displays throughout the year. I did not specially aim at variety, but, guided by the natural conditions of each region, tried to think out how best they might be fostered and perhaps a little bettered.

The only way in which variety of aspect was deliberately chosen was in the way of thinning out the natural growths. It was a wood of seedling trees that had come up naturally after an old wood of Scotch Fir had been cut down, and it seemed well to clear away all but one, or in some cases two kinds of trees in the several regions. Even in this the intention was to secure simplicity rather than variety, so that in moving about the ground there should be one thing at a time to see and enjoy. It is just this quality of singleness or simplicity of aim that I find wanting in gardens in general, where one may see quantities of the best plants grandly grown and yet no garden pictures.

Of course one has to remember that there are many minds to which this need of an artist's treatment of garden and woodland does not appeal, just as there are some who do not care for music or for poetry, or who see no difference between the sculpture of the old Greeks and that of any modern artist who is not of the first rank, or to whom architectural refinement is as an unknown language. And in the case of the more superficial enjoyment of flowers one has sympathy too. For a love of flowers, of any kind, however shallow, is a sentiment that makes for human sympathy and kindness, and is in itself uplifting, as everything must be that is a source of reverence and admiration. Still, the object of this book is to draw attention, however slightly and imperfectly, to the better ways of gardening, and to bring to bear upon the subject some consideration of that combination of common sense with sincerity of purpose, sense of beauty, and artistic knowledge that can make plain ground and growing things into a year-long succession of living pictures. Common sense I put first, because it restrains from any sort of folly or sham or affectation. Sense of beauty is the gift of God, for which those who have received it in good measure can never be thankful enough. The nurturing of this gift through long years of study, observation, and close application in any one of the ways in which fine art finds expression, is the training of the artist's brain and heart and hand. The better a human mind is trained to the perception of beauty the more opportunities will it find of exercising this precious gift, and the more directly will it be

DAFFODILS BY A WOODLAND PATH.

WILD PRIMROSES IN THIN WOODLAND.
(From a Picture by Henry Moon.)

brought to bear upon even the very simplest matters of everyday life, and always to their bettering.

So it was in the wood of young seedling trees, where Oak and Holly, Birch, Beech and Mountain Ash, came up together in a close thicket of young saplings. It seemed well to consider, in the first place, how to bring something like order into the mixed jumble, and, the better to do this, to appeal to the little trees themselves and see what they had to say about it.

The ground runs on a natural slope downward to the north, or, to be more exact, as the highest point is at one corner, its surface is tilted diagonally all over. So, beginning at the lower end of the woody growth, near the place where the house some day might stand, the first thing that appeared was a well-grown Holly, and rather near it, another ; both older trees than the more recent seedling growth. Close to the second Holly was a young Birch, the trunk about four inches thick and already in the early pride of its silvering bark. That was enough to prompt the decision that this part of the wood should be of silver Birch and Holly, so nearly all other growths were cut down or pulled up. A hundred yards higher up there were some strong young Oaks, then some Beeches, and all over the top of the ground a thick growth of young Scotch Fir, while the western region had a good sprinkling of promising Spanish Chestnut.

All these natural groupings were accepted, and a first thinning was made of the smallest stuff of other kinds. But it was done with the most careful watching, for there were to be no harsh frontiers. One kind of tree was to join hands with the next, though often a distinct deviation was made to the general rule. For the beautiful growth of the future wood was the thing that mattered, rather than obedience to any inflexible law.

Now, after twenty years, the saplings have become trees, and the preponderance of one kind of tree at a time has given a feeling of repose and dignity. Here and there something exceptional occurs, but it causes interest, not confusion. Five woodland walks pass upward through the trees ; every one has its own character, while the details change during its progress —never abruptly, but in leisurely sequence; as if inviting the quiet stroller to stop a moment to enjoy some little woodland suavity, and then gently enticing him to go further, with agreeable anticipation of what might come next. And if I may judge by the pleasure that these woodland ways give to some of my friends who I know are in sympathy with what I am trying to do, and by my own thankful delight in them, I may take it that my little sylvan pictures have come fairly right, so that I may ask my reader to go with me in spirit through some of them.

My house, a big cottage, stands facing a little to the east of south, just below the wood. The windows of the sitting-room, and its outer door, which stands open in all fine summer weather, look up a straight wide grassy way, the vista being ended by a fine old Scotch Fir with a background of dark wood. This old Fir and one other, and a number in and near the southern hedge, are all that remain of the older wood which was all of Scotch Fir.

THE WIDE WOOD-PATH.

CISTUS LAURIFOLIUS AT THE SUNNY ENTRANCE OF THE FERN WALK.

This green wood walk, being the widest and most important, is treated more boldly than the others— with groups of Rhododendrons in the region rather near the house, and for the rest only a biggish patch of the two North American Brambles, the white-flowered *Rubus nutkanus*, and the rosy *R. odoratus*. In spring the western region of tall Spanish Chestnuts, which begins just beyond the Rhododendrons, is carpeted with Poets' Narcissus ; the note of tender white blossom being taken up and repeated by the bloom-clouds of *Amelanchier*, that charming little woodland flowering tree whose use in such ways is so much neglected.   Close to the ground in the distance the light comes with brilliant effect through the young leaves of a .widespread carpet of Lily of the Valley, whose clusters of sweet little white bells will be a delight to see a month hence.

The Rhododendrons are carefully grouped for colour—pink, white, rose and red of the best qualities are in the sunniest part, while, kept well apart from them, near the tall Chestnuts and rejoicing in their partial shade, are the purple colourings, of as pure and cool a purple as may be found among carefully selected *ponticum* seedlings and the few named kinds that associate well with them.   Some details of this planting were given at length in my former book " Wood and Garden."

Among the Rhododendrons, at points carefully devised to be of good effect, either from the house or from various points of the lawn and grass paths, are strong groups of *Lilium auratum ;* they give a new picture of flower-beauty in the late summer and autumn and till near the end of October. The dark, strong foliage makes the best possible setting for the Lilies, and gives each group of them its fullest value. Another, narrower path, more to the east, is called the Fern walk, because, besides the general growth of Bracken that clothes the whole of the wood, there are groups of common hardy Ferns in easy patches, planted in such a way as to suggest that they grew there naturally. The Male Fern, the beautiful Dilated Shield Fern, and Polypody are native to the ground, and it was easy to place these, in some cases merely adding to a naturally grown tuft, so that they look quite at home. Lady Fern, *Blechnum* and *Osmunda*, and Oak and Beech Ferns have been added, the *Osmunda* in a depression that collects the water from any storms of rain. Later it was found that these wood-path edges offered suitable places for groups of the Willow Gentian (*G. asclepiadea*), and it was rather largely planted. It delights in a cool place in shade or half-shade, and when in September so many flowers are over and garden plants in general are showing evidence of fatigue and exhaustion, it is a pleasant thing to come upon a group of the arching sprays of this graceful and quite distinctive plant with its bright blue flowers an inch and a half long set in pairs in the axils of the willow-like leaves.

At the beginning of all these paths I took some pains to make the garden melt imperceptibly into the wood, and in each case to do it a different way. Where this path begins the lawn ends at a group of Oak, Holly, and Cistus, with an undergrowth of Gaultheria and Andromeda. The larger trees are to the left, and the small evergreen shrubs on a rocky mound to the right. Within a few yards the turf path becomes a true wood path. Just as wild gardening should never look like garden gardening, or, as it so sadly often does, like garden plants gone astray and quite out of place, so wood paths should never look like garden paths. There must be no hard edges, no obvious boundaries. The wood path is merely an easy way that the eye just perceives and the foot follows. It dies away imperceptibly on either side into the floor of the wood and is of exactly the same nature, only that it is smooth and easy and is not encumbered by projecting tree-roots, Bracken or Bramble, these being all removed when the path is made.

If it is open enough to allow of the growth of grass, and the grass has to be cut, and is cut with a machine, then a man with a faghook must follow to cut away slantingly the hard edge of standing grass that is left on each side. For the track of the machine not only leaves the hard, unlovely edges, but also brings into the wood the incongruous sentiment of that discipline of trimness which belongs to the garden, and that, even there in its own place, is often overdone.

Now we are in the true wood path among Oaks and Birches. Looking round, the view is here and there stopped by prosperous-looking Hollies, but for the most part one can see a fair way into the wood. In April the wood floor is plentifully furnished with Daffodils. Here, in the region furthest removed from

the white Poets' Daffodil of the upper ground, they
are all of trumpet kinds, and the greater number of
strong yellow colour.   For the Daffodils range through
the wood in a regular sequence of kinds that is not
only the prettiest way to have them, but that I have
often found, in the case of people who did not know
their Daffodils well, served to make the whole story
of their general kinds and relationships clear and
plain ; the hybrids of each group standing between
the parent kinds ; these again leading through other
hybrids to further clearly defined species, ending with
the pure trumpets.   As the sorts are intergrouped at
their edges, so that at least two removes are in view
at one time, the lesson in the general relationship of
kinds is easily learnt.

They are planted not in patches, but in long drifts;
a way that not only shows the plant in good number
to better advantage, but that is singularly happy in
its effect in the woodland landscape.   This is specially
noticeable towards the close of the day, when the
sunlight, yellowing as it nears the horizon, lights up
the long stretches of yellow bloom with an increase of
colour strength, while the wide-stretching shadow-
lengths throw the woodland shades into large *phrases*
of broadened mass, all subdued and harmonised by
the same yellow light that illuminates the long level
ranks of golden bloom.

From this same walk in June, looking westward
through the Birch stems, the value of the careful
colour scheme of the Rhododendrons is fully felt.
They are about a hundred yards away, and their mass

A WOOD-PATH AMONG CHESTNUTS.

A WOOD-PATH AMONG BIRCHES.

is broken by the groups of intervening tree-trunks; but their brightness is all the more apparent seen from under the nearer roofing mass of tree-top, and the yellowing light makes the intended colour-effect still more successful by throwing its warm tone over the whole.

But nearer at hand the Fern walk has its own little pictures. In early summer there are patches of *Trillium*, the white Wood Lily, in cool hollows among the ferns, and, some twenty paces further up, another wider group of the same. Between the two, spreading through a mossy bank, in and out among the ferns and right down to the path, next to a coming patch of Oak Fern, is a charming little white flower. Its rambling roots thread their way under the mossy carpet, and every few inches throw up a neat little stem and leaves crowned with a starry flower of tenderest white. It is *Trientalis*, a native of our most northern hill-woods, the daintiest of all woodland flowers.

To right and left white Foxgloves spire up among the Bracken. When the Foxglove seed is ripe, we remember places in the wood where tree-stumps were grubbed last winter. A little of the seed is scattered in these places and raked in. Meanwhile one forgets all about it, till two years afterwards there are the stately Foxgloves. It is good to see their strong spikes of solid bloom standing six to seven feet high, and then to look down again at the lowly *Trientalis* and to note how the tender little blossom, poised on its thread-like stem, holds its own in interest and importance.

B

Further up the Fern walk, near the upper group of *Trillium*, are some patches of a plant with roundish, glittering leaves. It is a North American *Asarum* (*A. virginicum*) ; the curious wax-like brown and greenish flower, after the usual manner of its kind, is short-stalked and hidden at the base of the leaf-stems. Near it, and growing close to the ground in a tuft of dark-green moss, is an interesting plant—*Goodyera epens*, a terrestrial Orchid. One might easily pass it by, for its curiously white-veined leaves are half hidden in the moss, and its spike of pale greenish-white flower is not conspicuous ; but, knowing it is there, I never pass without kneeling down, both to admire its beauty and also to ensure its well-being by a careful removal of a little of the deep moss here and there where it threatens too close an invasion.

Now there comes a break in the Fern walk, or rather it takes another character. The end of one of the wide green ways that we call the Lily path comes into it on the right, and immediately beyond this, stands the second of the great Scotch Firs of the older wood. The trunk, at five feet from the ground, has a girth of nine and a half feet. The colour of the rugged bark is a wonder of lovely tones of cool greys and greens, and of a luminous deep brown in the fissures and cavities. Where the outer layers have flaked off it is a warm reddish grey, of a quality that is almost peculiar to itself. This great tree's storm-rent head towers up some seventy feet, far above the surrounding foliage of Oak and Birch. Close to its foot, and showing

CISTUS CYPRIUS IN THE CISTUS CLEARING.

CISTUS BY THE WOOD-PATH.

behind it as one comes up the Fern walk, are a Holly and a Mountain Ash.

This spot is a meeting-place of several ways. On the right the wide green of the Lily path ; then, still bearing diagonally to the right, one of the paths into the region of Azalea and Cistus ; then, straight past the big tree, a wood walk carpeted with Whortleberry that passes through a whole Whortleberry region under Oaks, Hollies and Beeches; and, lastly, the path which is the continuation of the Fern walk. Looking along it one sees, a little way ahead, a closer shade of trees, for the most part Oak, but before entering this, on the right-hand gently rising bank, is a sheet of bright green leaves, closely set in May with neat spikes of white bloom. It is *Smilacina bifolia*, otherwise known as *Maianthemum bifolium*. The pretty little plant has taken to the place in a way that rejoices the heart of the wild gardener, joining in perfect accord with the natural growth of short Whortleberry and a background of the graceful fronds of Dilated Shield Fern, and looking as if it was of spontaneous growth.

Now the path passes a large Holly, laced through and through with wild Honeysuckle. The Honeysuckle stems that run up into the tree look like great ropes, and a quantity of the small ends come showering out of the tree-top and over the path, like a tangled veil of small cordage.

The path has been steadily rising, and now the ascent is a little steeper. The character of the trees is changing ; Oaks are giving way to Scotch Firs. Just where this change begins the bank to right and left is covered with the fresh, strong greenery of *Gaultheria Shallon*. About twenty years ago a few small pieces were planted. Now it is a mass of close green growth two to three feet high and thirty paces long, and extending for several yards into the wood to right and left. In a light, peaty soil such as this, it is the best of undershrubs. It is in full leaf-beauty in the dead of winter, while in early summer it bears clusters of good flowers of the Arbutus type. These are followed by handsome dark berries nearly as large as black currants, covered with a blue-grey bloom.

Now the path crosses another of the broad turfy ways, but here the turf is all of Heath ; a fourteen-foot-wide road of grey-rosy bloom in August ; and now we are in the topmost region of Scotch Fir, with undergrowth of Whortleberry.

The wood path next to this goes nearly straight up through the middle of the ground. It begins at another point of the small lawn next the house, and passes first by a turf walk through a mounded region of small shrubs and carefully placed pieces of the local sandstone. Andromeda, Skimmia and Alpenrose have grown into solid masses, so that the rocky ridges peer out only here and there. And when my friends say, " But then, what a chance you had with that shelf of rock coming naturally out of the ground," I feel the glowing warmth of an inward smile and think that perhaps the stones have not been so badly placed.

Near the middle of the woody ground a space was

GAULTHERIA SHALLON IN FLOWER.

GAULTHERIA SHALLON IN FRUIT.

cleared that would be large enough to be sunny throughout the greater part of the day. This was for Cistuses.
It is one of the compensations for gardening on the
poorest of soils that these delightful shrubs do well
with only the preparation of digging up and loosening
the sand, for my soil is nothing better. The kinds
that are best in the woody landscape are C. *laurifolius*
and C. *cyprius* ; *laurifolius* is the hardiest, *cyprius*
rather the more beautiful, with its three-and-a-half-
inch wide flowers of tenderest white with a red-purple
blotch at the base of each petal. Its growth, also, is
rather more free and graceful. It is the kind usually
sold as *ladaniferus*, and flowers in July. C. *laurifolius*
is a bush of a denser habit ; it bears an abundance
of bloom rather smaller than that of C. *cyprius*, and
without the coloured blotch. But when it grows old
and some of its stems are borne down and lie along
the ground, the habit changes and it acquires a free
pictorial character. These two large-growing Cistuses
are admirable for wild planting in sunny wood edges.
The illustrations (pp. 18 and 19) show their use, not only
in their own ground, but by the sides of the grassy
ways and the regions where the wood paths leave the
lawn.

The sheltered, sunny Cistus clearing has an undergrowth of wild heaths that are native to the ground,
but a very few other Heaths are added, namely, *Erica
ciliata* and the Cornish Heath ; and there is a fine
patch at the joining of two of the little grassy paths
of the white form of the Irish Heath (*Menziesia*, or
Daboëcia polifolia).

A project is in contemplation for a further extension of the clearing for the making of a heath garden, that promises to provide many happy hours of work in the coming winter.

WHITE IRISH HEATH.

THE SPRING GARDEN FROM D ON PLAN. "NEAR ROCK" IS TO THE LEFT.

CHAPTER III

THE SPRING GARDEN

As my garden falls naturally into various portions, distinct enough from each other to allow of separate treatment, I have found it well to devote one space at a time, sometimes mainly, sometimes entirely, to the flowers of one season of the year.

There is therefore one portion that is a complete little garden of spring flowers. It begins to show some bloom by the end of March, but its proper season is the month of April and three weeks of May.

In many places the spring garden has to give way to the summer garden, a plan that greatly restricts the choice of plants, and necessarily excludes some of the finest flowers of the early year.

My spring garden lies at the end and back of a high wall that shelters the big summer flower border from the north and north-west winds. The line of the wall is continued as a Yew hedge that in time will rise to nearly the same height, about eleven feet. At the far end the Yew hedge returns to the left so as to fence in the spring flowers from the east and to hide some sheds. The space also encloses some beds of Tree Peonies and a plot of grass, roughly circular in shape, about eight yards across, which is nearly surrounded

23

by Oaks, Hollies and Cob-nuts. The plan shows its
disposition. It is of no design ; the space was accepted
with its own conditions, arranged in the simplest way
as to paths, and treated very carefully for colour. It
really makes as pretty a picture of spring flowers as
one could wish to see.

The chief mass of colour is in the main border. The
circles marked V and M are strong plants of Veratrum
and Myrrhis. Gardens of spring flowers generally have
a thin, poor effect for want of plants of important
foliage. The greater number of them look what they
are—temporary makeshifts. It seemed important
that in this little space, which is given almost entirely
to spring flowers, this weakness should not be allowed.
But herbaceous plants of rather large growth with fine
foliage in April and May are not many. The best I
could think of are *Veratrum nigrum*, *Myrrhis odorata*
and the newer *Euphorbia Wulfenii*. The *Myrrhis* is
the Sweet Cicely of old English gardens. It is an um-
belliferous plant with large fern-like foliage, that makes
early growth and flowers in the beginning of May. At
three years old a well-grown plant is a yard high and
across. After that, if the plants are not replaced by
young ones, they grow too large, though they can be
kept in check by a careful removal of the outer leaves
and by cutting out some whole crowns when the plant
is making its first growth. The Veratrum, with its
large, deeply plaited, undivided leaves, is in striking
contrast, but the two kinds of plants, in groups as the
plan shows, with running patches of the large form of
Megasea cordifolia, the great *Euphorbia Wulfenii* and

PLAN OF THE SPRING GARDEN

some groups of Black Hellebore, just give that comfortable impression of permanence and distinct intention that are usually so lamentably absent from gardens of spring flowers.

Many years ago I came to the conclusion that in all flower borders it is better to plant in long rather than block-shaped patches. It not only has a more pictorial effect, but a thin long planting does not leave an unsightly empty space when the flowers are done and the leaves have perhaps died down. The word " drift " conveniently describes the shape I have in mind, and I commonly use it in speaking of these long-shaped plantings.

Such drifts are shown faintly in the plan, reduced in number and simplified in form, but serving to show the general manner of planting. There are of course many plants that look best in a distinct clump or even as single examples, such as *Dictamnus* (the Burning Bush), and the beautiful pale yellow *Pæonia wittmanniana*, a single plant of which is marked W near the beginning of the main border.

For the first seven or eight yards, in the front and middle spaces, there are plants of tender colouring— pale Primroses, Tiarella, pale yellow Daffodils, pale yellow early Iris, pale lemon Wallflower, double Arabis, white Anemones and the palest of the lilac Aubrietias ; also a beautiful pale lilac Iris, one of the Caparne hybrids ; with long drifts of white and pale yellow Tulips—nothing deeper in colour than the graceful *Tulipa retroflexa*. At the back of the border the colours are darker; purple Wallflower and the great dull red-

THE FERN-LIKE SWEET CICELY.

THE SPRING GARDEN FROM E ON PLAN. "FURTHER ROCK" IS ON THE NEAR RIGHT HAND.

purple double Tulip so absurdly called Bleu Céleste. These run through and among and behind the first clump of Veratrums.

In the middle of the length of the border there is still a good proportion of tender and light colouring in front : white Primroses and Daffodils ; the pale yellow Uvularia and *Adonis vernalis ;* but with these there are stronger colours: Tulip Chrysolora of fuller yellow, yellow Wallflowers, the tall Doronicum, and, towards the back, several patches of yellow Crown Imperial.

Then again in front, with more double Arabis, is the lovely pale blue of *Myosotis dissitiflora* and *Mertensia virginica*, and, with sheets of the foam-like Tiarella, the tender pink of *Dicentra eximia* and pink and rose-red Tulips. At the back of this come scarlet Tulips, the stately cream-white form of *Camassia Leichtlini* and a bold tuft of Solomon's Seal ; then Orange Tulips, brown Wallflowers, Orange Crown Imperial, and taller scarlet Tulips of the *gesneriana* class. The strong colouring is repeated beyond the cross-path where the patches of Acanthus are shown, with more orange Tulips, brown Wallflowers, orange Crown Imperial and great flaming scarlet *gesneriana* Tulips. All this shows up finely against the background of dark yew. At the extreme end, where the yew hedge returns forward at a right angle, this point is accentuated by a raised mound of triangular shape, dry-walled and slightly curved forward on the side facing the border and the spectator. On this at the back is a young plant of *Yucca gloriosa* for display in future years and a front planting of the large growing *Euphorbia Wulfenii*, one of the grandest and most pictorial of plants of recent acquirement for garden use.

The Acanthus and Yucca are of course plants of middle and late summer ; between them are some Tritomas. These plants are here because one of the most often used of the garden thoroughfares passes the point C, which is a thick-roofed arch of Rose and Clematis, and, seen from this point and framed by the near greenery, they form a striking picture of middle-distant form and colour in the later summer.

The space marked Further Rock is an upward-sloping bank, the Hollies standing on rather higher ground. Here the plants are between, and tumbling over, rocky ridges. Next the large Holly, and extending to the middle of the rocky promontory, are again the strong reds and browns, with accompanying bronze-red foliage of *Heuchera Richardsoni.* This gives place to dark green carpeting masses of Iberis with cold-white bloom, and, nearer the path, *Lithospermum prostratum ;* the flower-colour here changing, through white, to blue and bluish ; *Myosotis* in front telling charmingly against the dark-leaved *Lithospermum.* At the highest points, next to a great crowning bo·'lder, is the Common Blue Iris and a paler one of the beautiful Caparne series. Then down to the path where it begins to turn is a drift of the bluish-lilac *Phlox divaricata,* and, opposite the cross-path, some jewels of the newer pale yellow *Alyssum sulphureum.* This rocky shoulder is also enlivened by a natural-looking but very carefully considered planting of white Tulips that run through both the blue and the red regions.

The corner marked Near Rock is also a slightly raised bank. The dark dots are cob-nuts ; the dotted line between is where there are garlands of *Clematis montana* that swing on ropes between the nuts. The garlands dip down and nearly meet the flowers of some pale pink Tree Peonies. Open spaces above the garlands and under the meeting branches of the nuts give glimpses of distant points where some little scheme has been devised to please the eye, such as the bit of bank to the left of Seat A, where there are two little fish-like drifts of palest Aubrietia in a dense grey setting of Cerastium.

The point of the Near Rock next the path agrees with the colouring opposite, but also has features of its own ; a groundwork of grey *Antennaria*, the soft lilac-pink of the good *Aubrietia Moorheimi* changing to the left to the fuller pink of *Phlox amœna*, and above to the type colour of Aubrietia and some of the strong purples such as the variety Dr. Mules. To the left, towards the oaks, the colouring is mostly purple, with stout tufts of the Spring Bitter Vetch (*Orobus vernus*), purple Wallflowers, and, under and behind the nuts, purple Honesty. Thin streams of white Tulips intermingle with other streams of pink Tulips that crown the angle and flow down again to the main path between ridges of double Arabis, white Iberis, and cloudy masses of the pretty pale yellow *Corydalis ochroleuca*, which spreads into a wide carpet under the Tree Peonies and Clematis garlands.

Further along, just clear of the nuts, are some patches of *Dielytra spectabilis*, its graceful growth arching out over the lower stature of pink Tulips and harmonising charmingly with the pinkish-green foliage of the Tree Peonies just behind. The pink Tulips are here in some quantity; they run boldly into pools of pale blue Myosotis, with more Iberis where the picture demands the strongest, deepest green, and more Corydalis where the softer, greyer tones will make it better.

The space marked Shade, always in shade from the nuts and oaks, is planted with rather large patches of the handsome white-flowered *Dentaria*, the graceful North American *Uvularia grandiflora*, in habit like a small Solomon's Seal, but with yellow flowers much larger in proportion; with Myrrhis and purple Honesty at the back and sheets of Sweet Woodruff to the front.

There are Tree Peonies in the long border and the two others. It is difficult to grow them in my hot, dry, sandy soil, even though I make them a liberal provision of just such a compost as I think they will like. I have noticed that they do best when closely overshadowed by some other growing thing. In the two near beds there are some Mme. Alfred Carrière Roses that are trained to arch over to the angles, so as to comfort and encourage the Peonies. These beds have an informal edging of *Stachys lanata*, one of the most useful of plants for grey effects. Through it come white Tulips in irregular patches.

The long border has also Tree Peonies planted about two and a half feet from the edge. Partly to give the bed a sort of backbone, and partly to shelter the Tree Peonies, it has some bushes of *Veronica Traversi* and one or two *Leycesteria formosa*. In the middle of the

"FURTHER ROCK," FROM **Q** *ON PLAN.*

"FURTHER ROCK" FROM H ON PLAN: IBERIS, PHLOX STELLARIA AND PHLOX DIVARICATA, WHITE TULIPS AND BLUE IRIS.

length is a clump of *Lilium giganteum* and a biggish grouping of *Dielytra spectabilis*. All along the outer border there are patches and long straggling groups of the pretty dwarf Irises of the *pumila, olbiensis* and *chamæ-iris* sections, with others of the same class of stature and habit. Any bare spaces are filled with Wallflowers and Honesty in colours that accord with the general arrangement. The narrow border has mostly small shrubs, Berberis and so on, forming one mass with the hedge to the left, which consists of a double dry wall about four feet high, with earth between and a thick growth on the top of Berberis, *Rosa lucida* and Scotch Briers. Except the Berberis these make no show of flower within the blooming time of the spring garden, but the whole is excellent as a background.

Red primroses are in the narrow border next to the cross-wall ; the wall here is much lower than the longer one on the right. The Primroses are grouped with the reddish-leaved *Heuchera Richardsoni*, the two together making a rich colour-harmony. Beyond them are scarlet Tulips. The small shaded rounds in this border and its continuation across the path into the near end of the main border are stout larch posts supporting a strong growth of Rose Mme. Alfred Carrière and *Clematis montana*. These have grown together into a solid continuously intermingling mass, the path at C passing under a low arch of their united branches. The high wall on the right is also covered with flowering things of the early year, Morella Cherries, *Rubus deliciosus* and *Clematis montana*, some of this foaming over from the other side of the wall.

The wall is a part, about a third of the length, of the high wall that protects the large border of summer and autumn flowers from the north, and that forms the dividing-line between the pleasure garden proper and the working garden beyond.

On the plan are letters with arrows referring to the illustrations. The letter is at the spot where the camera stood ; the arrow points to the middle of the picture. Thus the one taken from D shows two-thirds of the longest path with the end of the big wall and the Yew hedge that prolongs its line on the right and the Nut-trees on the left. The colouring on the right is of pale purple Aubrietia and double white Arabis, with pale Daffodils, and, at the back, groups of sulphur Crown Imperial.

The more distant colouring is of brown Wallflower and red Tulip and the bright mahogany-coloured Crown Imperial. The picture from E is done from among the reds and strong yellows and looks to point C, and further, through the arch of Rose and Clematis, to the summer garden beyond. The other illustrations show groups of colouring more in detail. The one from F looks at Near Rock from one side. Over the grey Stachys and its milk-white Tulips is seen the flowery mass of pale and deep lilac, and pinkish lilac with grey foliage, crowned with pink and white Tulips near the foot of the Nuts. The picture from G looks at the bit of bank called Further Rock with its big piece of sandstone that looks as if it came naturally out of the ground. Here is a mass of dead-white Iberis with Tulips of a softer white, then the

"NEAR ROCK" FROM **F** ON PLAN : AUBRIETIAS, PHLOX AMŒNA AND WHITE AND PINK TULIP.

THE PRIMROSE GARDEN.

lilac-white of *Phlox stellaria* and the bluish lilac of *Phlox divaricata*. The picture from H was done a few days later. It shows the further mass of *Phlox divaricata* more fully in bloom, and among the white Tulips above, a pretty pale lilac-blue hybrid Iris and some taller stems of the common Blue Flag Iris just coming into blossom. This picture shows the value of the dark Yew hedge as a background to the flowers. Just at the back of the flowery bank are Hollies, and then the hedge. This has not yet come to its full height and the top still shows a ragged outline, but in two years' time it will have grown into shape.

The Primrose garden is in a separate place among Oaks and Hazels. It is for my special strain of large yellow and white bunch Primroses, now arrived at a state of fine quality and development by a system of careful seed-selection that has been carried on for more than thirty years.

CHAPTER IV

BETWEEN SPRING AND SUMMER

WHEN the Spring flowers are done, and before the full June days come with the great Flag Irises and the perennial Lupines, there is a kind of mid-season. If it can be given a space of ground it will be well bestowed. I have a place that I call the Hidden Garden, because it is in a corner that might so easily be overlooked if one did not know where to find it. No important path leads into it, though two pass within ten yards of it on either side. It is in a sort of clearing among Ilex and Holly, and the three small ways into it are devious and scarcely noticeable from the outside. The most important of these, marked 1 on the plan, passes between some clumps of over-arching Bamboo and through a short curved tunnel of Yew and Ilex. Another, marked 2, is only just traceable among Berberis under a large Birch, and comes sharply round a tall Monterey Cypress. The third turns out of one of the shady woodland glades and comes into the little garden by some rough stone steps.

The plan shows the simple arrangement, the paths following the most natural lines that the place suggests. The main path goes down some shallow, rough stone steps with a sunny bank to the left and a rocky mound

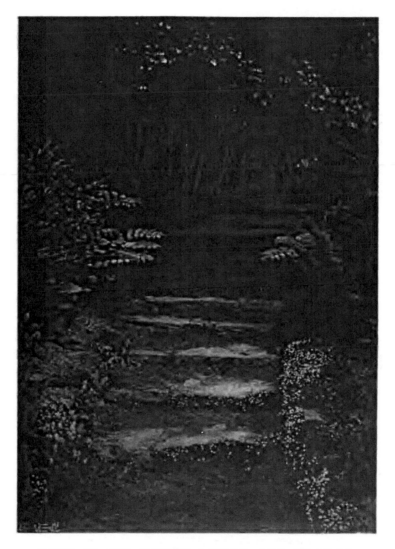

STEPS TO THE HIDDEN GARDEN AT **3** *ON PLAN.*

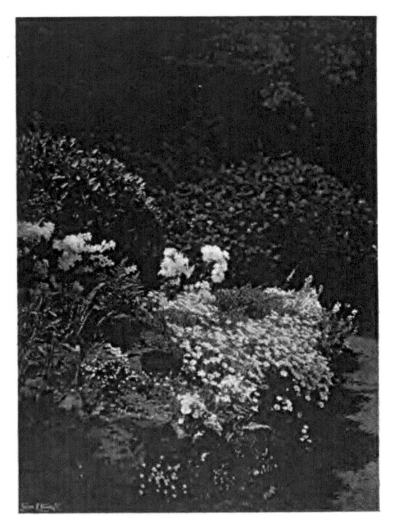

PHLOX DIVARICATA AND ARENARIA MONTANA.

to the right. The mound is crowned with small shrubs, Alpine Rhododendrons and Andromeda. Both this and the left-hand bank have a few courses of rough dry-walling next the path on its lowest level. A little cross-path curves into the main one from the right.

The path leaves the garden again by a repetition of the rough stone steps. The mossy growth of *Arenaria balearica* clings closely to the stones on their cooler faces, and the frond-like growths of Solomon's Seal hang out on either side as a fitting prelude to the dim mysteries of the wide green wood path beyond.

It is a garden for the last days of May and the first fortnight of June.

Passing through the Yew tunnel, the little place bursts on the sight with good effect. What is most striking is the beauty of the blue-lilac *Phlox divaricata* and that of two clumps of Tree Peony—the rosy Baronne d'Alès and the pale salmon-pink Comtesse de Tuder. The little garden, with its quiet environment of dark foliage, forbids the use of strong colouring, or perhaps one should say that it suggested a restriction of the scheme of colouring to the tenderer tones. There seemed to be no place here for the gorgeous Oriental Poppies, although they too are finest in partial shade, or for any strong yellows, their character needing wider spaces and clearer sunlight.

The Tree Peonies are in two groups of the two kinds only ; it seemed enough for the limited space. In front of Comtesse de Tuder is a group of *Funkia Sieboldi*, its bluish leaves harmonising delightfully with the leaf-colour of the Peonies ; next to them is a corner of glistening deep green Asarum. No other flowers of any size are near, but there are sheets of the tender yellow bloom and pale foliage of *Corydalis ochroleuca*, of the white-bloomed Woodruff, and the pale green leafage of Epimedium ; and among them tufts of Lent Hellebores, also in fresh young leaf, and a backing of the feathery fronds of Lady Fern and of the large Solomon's Seal ; with drooping garlands of *Clematis montana* hanging informally from some rough branching posts. Yew-trees are at the back, and then Beeches in tender young leaf.

The foot of the near mound is a pink cloud of London Pride. Shooting up among it and just beyond is the white St. Bruno's Lily. More of this lovely little lily-like Anthericum is again a few feet further along, grouped with *Iris Cengialti*, one of the bluest of the Irises. The back of the mound has some of the tenderly tinted Caparne hybrid Irises two feet high, of pale lilac colouring, rising from among dark-leaved, white-bloomed Iberis, and next the path a pretty, large-flowered Tufted Pansy that nearly matches the Iris.

But the glory of the mound is the long stretch of blue-lilac *Phlox divaricata*, whose colour is again repeated by a little of the same on the sunny bank to the left. Here it is grouped with pale pink Scotch Brier, more pale yellow Corydalis and *Arenaria montana* smothered in its masses of white bloom. At the end of the bank the colour of the *Phlox divaricata* is deepened by sheaves of *Camassia esculenta* that spear up through it. The whole back of this bank has a free planting

MALE FERN IN THE HIDDEN GARDEN.

EXOCHORDA GRANDIFLORA.

PLAN OF THE HIDDEN GARDEN.

of graceful pale-coloured Columbines with long spurs, garden kinds that come easily from seed and that were originally derived from some North American species. They are pale yellow and warm white ; some have the outer portion of the flower of a faint purple, much like that of some of the patches in an old, much-washed, cotton patchwork quilt.

The dark trees on the right have rambling Roses growing into them—Paul's Carmine Pillar and the Himalayan *R. Brunonis*. The red Rose does not flower so freely here as on a pillar in sunlight, but its fewer stems clamber high into the Holly, and the bloom shows in thin natural wreaths that are even more pleasing to an artist's eye than the more ordered abundance of the flowery post. At the foot of the Hollies hardy Ferns grow luxuriantly in the constant shade. A little later a few clumps of Lilies will spring up from among them ; the lovely pink *rubellum*, the fine yellow *szovitzianum*, and the buff *testaceum*.

On the left-hand side, behind the sunny bank, a Garland Rose comes through and tumbles out of a Yew, and some sprays of an old bush of the single *R. poly-antha*, that has spread to a circumference of one hundred and fifty feet, have pushed their way through the Ilex.

The Hollies and Ilexes all round are growing fast, and before many years are over the little garden will become too shady for the well-being of the flowers that now occupy it. It will then change its character and become a Fern garden.

All gardening involves constant change. It is even more so in woodland. A young bit of wood such as mine is for ever changing. Happily, each new development reveals new beauty of aspect or new possibility of good treatment, such as, rightly apprehended and then guided, tends to a better state than before.

Meanwhile the little tree-embowered garden has a quiet charm of its own. It seems to delight in its character of a Hidden Garden, and in the pleasant surprise that its sudden discovery provokes. For between it and its owner there is always a pretty little play of pretending that there is no garden there, and of being much surprised and delighted at finding, not only that there is one, but quite a pretty one.

The Hidden Garden is so small in extent, and its boundaries are already so well grown, that there is no room for many of the beautiful things of the time of year. For May is the time for the blooming of the most important of our well-known flowering shrubs—Lilac, Guelder Rose, White Broom, Laburnum, and *Pyrus Malus floribunda*. But one shrub, as beautiful as any of these and as easily grown, seems to be forgotten. This is *Exochorda grandiflora*—related to the Spiræas. Its pearl-like buds have earned it the name of Pearl Bush, but its whole lovely bloom should before now have secured it a place in every good garden.

Every one knows the Guelder Rose, with its round white flower-balls, but the wild shrub of which this is a garden variety is also a valuable ornamental bush and should not be neglected. It is a native plant, growing in damp places, such as the hedges of water-meadows and the sides of streams. The English name

EUPHORBIA WULFENII.

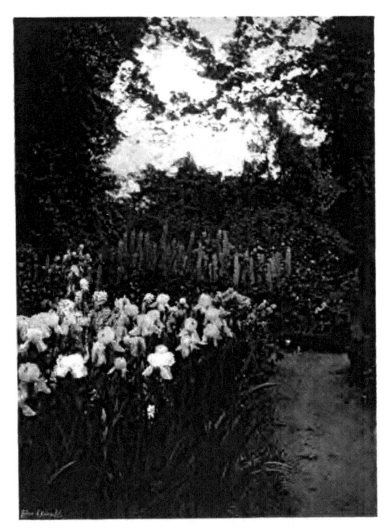

IRISES AND LUPINES IN THE JUNE GARDEN.

is Water Elder. Its merit as a garden shrub does not lie, as in the Guelder Rose, in its bloom, but in its singularly beautiful fruit. This, in autumn, lights up the whole shrub with a ruddy radiance. Grown on drier ground than that of its natural habitat, it takes a closer, more compact form.

White Broom is in flower from the middle of May to the second week of June. There is a fine Flag Iris of a rich purple colour called " Purple King." It is well to grow it just in front of some young bushes of White Broom. Then, if one of the hybrid Irises of pale lilac colour is there as well, and a bush of *Rosa altaica*, the colour-effect will be surprisingly beautiful. This Rose is the bolder-growing, Asiatic equivalent of our Burnet Rose (*R. spinosissima*), with the same lemon-white flowers. When any such group containing White Broom is planted, it should be remembered that the tendency of the Broom is to grow tall and leggy. It bears pruning, but it is a good plan to plant some extra ones behind the others. After a couple of years, if the front plants have grown out of bounds, the back ones can be bent down and fastened to sticks, so that their heads come in the required places. It is one of the many ways in which a pretty garden picture may be maintained from year to year by the exercise of a little thought and ingenuity. The undergrowth of such a group may be of Solomon's Seal at the back, and, if the bank or border is in sun, of a lower groundwork of Iberis and *Corydalis ochroleuca*, or, if it is shaded, of Tiarella, Woodruff or *Anemone sylvestris*. With these, for the sake of their tender green foliage, there may well be *Uvularia grandiflora* and *Epimedium pinnatum*. There is now a dwarf form of the White Broom, a plant not only less in height but of a more close and compact shape, that is useful for grouping in front of the older, taller one as well as for use in places where the original plant is too large.

A wonderful plant of May is the great *Euphorbia Wulfenii*. It adapts itself to many ways of use, for, though the immense yellow-green heads of bloom are at their best in May, they are still of pictorial value in June and July, while the deep-toned, grey-blue foliage is in full beauty throughout the greater part of the year. It is valuable in boldly arranged flower borders, and holds its own among shrubs of moderate size, but I always think its best use would be in the boldest kind of rock-work.

One of my desires that can never be fulfilled is to have a rocky hill-side in full sun, so steep as to be almost precipitous, with walls of bare rock only broken by ledges that can be planted. I would have great groups of Yucca standing up against the sky and others in the rock-face, and some bushes of this great *Euphorbia* and only a few other plants, all of rather large grey effect; *Phlomis*, Lavender, Rosemary and Cistus, with *Othonna* hanging down in long sheets over the bare face of the warm rock. It would be a rock-garden on an immense scale, planted as Nature plants, with not many different things at a time. The restriction to a few kinds of plants would give the impression of spontaneous growth; of that large, free, natural effect that is so rarely achieved in artificial planting. Besides natural hill-sides, there must be old quarries within or near the pleasure-grounds of many places in our islands where such a scheme of planting could worthily be carried out.

CHAPTER V

THE JUNE GARDEN

BEYOND the lawn and a belt of Spanish Chestnut I have a little cottage that is known as the Hut. I lived in it for two years while my house was building, and may possibly live in it again for the sake of replenishing an over-drained exchequer, if the ideal well-to-do invalid flower-lover or some such very quiet summer tenant, to whom alone I could consent to surrender my dear home for a few weeks, should be presented by a kind Providence. Meanwhile it is always in good use for various purposes, such as seed-drying, *pot-pourri* preparing, and the like.

The garden in front and at the back is mainly a June garden. It has Peonies, Irises, Lupines, and others of the best flowers of the season, and a few for later blooming. The entrance to the Hut is through Yews that arch overhead. Close to the right is a tall Holly with a *Clematis montana* growing into it and tumbling out at the top. The space of garden to the left, being of too deep a shape to be easily got at from the path on the one side and the stone paving on the other, has a kind of dividing backbone made of a double row of Rose hoops or low arches, rising from good greenery of Male Fern and the fern-like Sweet

CERASTIUM AS AN INFORMAL EDGING.

*PART OF THE GARLAND ROSE AT THE ANGLE OF THE
HUT GARDEN.*

Cicely. This handsome plant (*Myrrhis odorata*) is of
great use in many ways. It will grow anywhere,
and has the unusual merit of making a good show of
foliage quite early in the year. It takes two years
to get to a good size, sending its large, fleshy, aromatic
roots deep down into the soil. By the end of May,
when the bloom is over and the leaves are full grown,
they can be cut right down, when the plant will at
once form a new set of leaves that remain fresh for the
rest of the summer. Its chief use is as a good foliage
accompaniment or background to flowers, and no plant
is better for filling up at the bases of shrubs that look
a little leggy near the ground, or for any furnishing
of waste or empty spaces, especially in shade. From
among the Ferns and Myrrhis at the back of this bit
of eastern border rise white Foxgloves, the great white
Columbine, and the tall stems of white Peach-leaved
Campanula. Nearer to the front are clumps of
Peonies. But, as one of the most frequented paths
passes along this eastern border, it was thought best
not to confine it to June flowers only, but to have
something also for the later months. All vacant
places are therefore filled with Pentstemons and Snapdragons, which make a show throughout the summer ;
while for the early days of July there are clumps of the
old garden Roses—Damask and Provence. The whole
south-western angle is occupied by a well-grown
Garland Rose that every summer is loaded with its
graceful wreaths of bloom. It has never been trained
or staked, but grows as a natural fountain ; the
branches are neither pruned nor shortened. The only

attention it receives is that every three or four years the internal mass of old dead wood is cut right out, when the bush seems to spring into new life.

Passing this angle and going along the path leading to the studio door in the little stone-paved court, there is a seat under an arbour formed by the Yews ; the front of it has a Dundee Rambler Rose supported by a rough wooden framework. On the right, next the paving, are two large standard Roses with heads three and four feet through. They are old garden Roses, worked in cottage fashion on a common Dog-rose stock. One is Céleste, of loveliest tender rose colour, its broad bluish leaves showing its near relationship to *Rosa alba ;* the other the white Mme. Plantier. This old Rose, with its abundant bunches of pure white flowers, always seems to me to be one of the most charming of the older garden kinds. It will grow in almost any way, and is delightful in all ; as a pillar, as a hedge, as a bush, as a big cottage standard, or in the border tumbling about among early summer flowers. Like the Blush Gallica, which just precedes it in time of blooming, it is one of the old picture Roses. Both should be in quantity in every garden, and yet they are but rarely to be seen.

The border next the paving has clumps of the old garden Peonies (*P. officinalis*). By the time these are over, towards the end of June, groups of the earlier orange Herring Lilies are in bloom. A thick and rather high Box edging neatly trims these borders, and favours the cottage-garden sentiment that is fostered in this region. At the back of the Yews that

ROSE BLUSH GALLICA PLANTED ON THE TOP OF
DRY WALLING.

SPANISH IRIS.

form the arbour is one end of the Hidden Garden. Going along the path, past the projection on the block-plan of the Hut, which represents the large ingle of the studio, we come to the other bit of June garden behind the little cottage. Here again, the space being over-wide, it is divided in the middle by a double border of Rosemary that is kept clipped and is not allowed to rise high enough to prevent access to the border on each side.

On the side next the Hut the flowers are mostly of lilac and purple colouring with white. Pale lilac Irises, including the fine *I. Pallida dalmatica* and the rosy-lilac variety, Queen of the May; perennial Lupines, white, bluish lilac and purple—one of a conspicuous and rare deep red-purple of extreme richness without the slightest taint of a rank quality—a colour I can only call a strong wine-purple; then a clump of the feathery, ivory-white *Spiræa Aruncus*, the large Meadowsweet that is so fine by the side of alpine torrents. There are also some flesh-pink Albiflora Peonies and lower growths of Catmint, and of the grand blue-purple Cranesbill, *Geranium ibericum platy-phyllum*, with white and pale yellow Spanish Irises in generous tufts springing up between. At the blunt angle nearly opposite the dovecote is a pink cloud of London Pride; beyond it pale yellow Violas with more white Spanish Iris, leading to a happy combination of the blue *Iris Cengialti* and the bushy Aster *Olearia Gunni*, smothered in its white starry bloom. An early flowering Flag Iris, named Chamæleon, nearly matches the colour of *I. Cengialti;* it is the bluest that I know of the Flag Irises, and is planted between and around the Olearias to form part of the colour-picture.

Beyond this group, and only separated from it by some pale yellow Irises, are two plants of the Dropmore Anchusa Opal, marked A on the plan, of pure pale blue, and another clump of *Spiræa Aruncus*, marked S, and one of a good pure white Lupine, with some tall clear yellow Irises and white Foxgloves. Now the colouring changes, passing through a group or two of the rich half-tones of Irises of the *squalens* section to the perennial Poppies ; *P. rupifragum* nearest the path and, next to it, *P. pilosum :* both of a rich apricot colour. Backing these is a group of the larger hybrid that nearly always occurs in gardens where there are both *P. rupifragum* and *P. orientale*. In appearance it is a small *orientale* with a strong look of *rupifragum* about the foliage. As a garden plant it has the advantages of being of an intermediate size and of having a long season of bloom, a quality no doubt inherited from *rupifragum*, which will flower more or less throughout the summer if the seed-pods are removed. A plant of Oriental Poppy of the tone of orange-scarlet that I know as red-lead colour, and some deep orange Lilies complete this strongly coloured group.

In the north-western clump, where there are some Thorn-trees and two Thuyas, the dominant feature is the great bush of an old garden rambling Rose that looks as if its parentage was somewhere between *sempervirens* and *arvensis*. I can neither remember how I came by it nor match it with any nursery kind,

It stands nearly opposite the Hut kitchen window, and when in full bloom actually sheds light into the room. I know it as the Kitchen Rose. The diameter of the bush is even greater than the plan shows, for it overwhelms the nearest Thuya and rushes through the Thorn, and many of its shoots are within hand-reach of the back path. The rest of this clump is occupied by plants of tall habit—the great Mullein (*Verbascum orientale*), the Giant Cow-Parsnip (*Heracleum Mantegazzianum*), and white Foxgloves.

The plan shows how the border of early bulbs, described in a former chapter (now a mass of hardy Ferns, as shown at p. 7), lies in relation to this part of the garden. There is also a grand mass of Oriental Poppy and Orange Lilies in half-shade on the other side of the path, where it turns and is bordered with Berberis. This makes a fine distant effect of strong colour looking north-west from the southern end of the bulb-border.

I greatly wish I could have some other June borders for the still better use of the Flag Irises, but not only have I quite as much dressed ground as I can afford to keep up, but the only space where such borders could be made has to be nursery-ground of plants for sale. But though I am denied this pleasure myself, I should like to suggest it to others, and therefore give plans of two borders of different colourings. There would be no great harm if they came opposite each other, though perhaps, as colour schemes, they would be rather better seen singly and quite detached from each other.

It must be remembered, as in all cases of planting flower borders, that they cannot be expected to show their full beauty the year after planting. Irises will give a few blooms the first season, but are not in strength till their second and third years. China Roses must have time to grow. Tree Lupines must be planted young, and though they make rapid growth, they also do not fill their spaces till the third year. Lupine Somerset is a desirable hybrid, not quite a true Tree Lupine, though it has a half-woody growth. Its best colour is a clear, lively light yellow, but it readily varies from seed to whitish or washy purplish tints. As the seedlings often show bloom the first season in the seed-bed, the colours should be noted and marked, for some of the light purples are pretty things, with more refinement of character than the same colourings in the old Tree Lupines. Both the tree and hybrid kinds may have their lives much prolonged—for if they are not specially treated they are short-lived things—by judicious pruning. After flowering, each branch should be cut well back. It is not enough to cut away the flowers, but every branch should be shortened about two-thirds as soon as the bloom is over and the seed-pods begin to form.

The plans show the two schemes of colouring. The upper is of white, lilac, purple and pink, with grey foliage ; the lower of white, yellow, bronze-yellow and, for the most part, rich green foliage. They will show mainly as Iris and Lupine borders, and are intended to display the beauty of these two grand plants of early summer. The kinds of Iris are

WHITE TREE LUPINE.

CATMINT IN JUNE IN THE GREY AUGUST BORDER.

carefully considered for their height, time of blooming and colour value. In the yellow border is one patch of clear, pale pure blue, the Dropmore Anchusa Opal, grouped with pale yellows and white.

In the purple border are some important front-edge patches of the beautiful Catmint (*Nepeta Mussini*), a plant that can hardly be over-praised. The illustration shows it in a part of a border-front that is to be for August. For a good three weeks in June it makes this border a pretty place, although the Catmint is its only flower. But with the white-grey woolly patches of Stachys and the half-grown bushes of Gypsophila, and the Lavender and other plants of greyish foliage, the picture is by no means incomplete. Its flowery masses, seen against the warm yellow of the sandy path, give the impression of remarkably strong and yet delightfully soft colouring. The colour itself is a midway purple, between light and dark, of just the most pleasing quality. As soon as the best of the bloom is done it is carefully cut over ; then the lateral shoots just below the main flower-spike that has been taken out will gain strength and bloom again at the border's best show-time in August. In another double flower border that is mostly for the September-blooming Michaelmas Daisies the Catmint is cut back a little later.

One of the joys of June is the beauty of the Scotch Briars. On the south side of the house there are Figs and Vines, Rosemary and China Roses, and then a path, from which easy stone steps lead up to the strip of lawn some fifty feet wide that skirts the wood. To right and left of the steps, for a length equal to that of the house-front, is a hedge of these charming little Roses. They are mostly double white, but some are rosy and some yellow. When it is not in flower the mass of small foliage is pleasant to see, and even in winter leaflessness the tangle of close-locked branches has an appearance of warm brown comfort that makes it good to have near a house.

June is also the time of some of the best of the climbing plants and slightly tender shrubs that we have against walls and treat as climbers, such as *Solanum crispum* and *Abutilon vitifolium* and the hardy *Clematis montana*; but some notes on these will be offered in a further chapter.

One is always watching and trying for good combinations of colour that occur or that may be composed. Besides such as are shown in the plans, the following have been noted for June :

In rock-work the tiny China Rose Pompon de Paris, also the tender pink Fairy Rose, with pale lilac Tufted Pansy and *Achillea umbellata*.

The pretty pale pink dwarf Rose Mignonette, with the lilac of Catmint (*Nepeta Mussini*) and the grey-white foliage of Stachys and *Cineraria maritima*.

In a cool, retired place in a shrubbery margin, away from other flowers, the misty red-grey-purple of *Thalictrum aquilegifolium purpureum* with the warm white foam-colour of *Spiræa Aruncus*.

On bold rock-work, a mass of a fine-coloured strain of Valerian (*Centranthus*) with a deep scarlet-crimson

SCOTCH BRIARS.

GERANIUM IBERICUM PLATYPHYLLUM: THE BEST OF THE CRANEBILLS.

(See page 45.)

Snapdragon. This is a success of reciprocally enhancing texture as well as colour ; the texture having that satisfying quality that one recognises in the relation of the cut and uncut portions of the fine old Italian cut-velvets.

In April Campernelle Jonquil with *Myosotis dissitiflora*.

In May the true *Pulmonaria azurea* with the white form of *Scilla italica*.

In a shrubbery edge, or some cool, half shady place, the purple form of *Thalictrum aquilegifolium* with white Foxgloves, and in the same kind of place *Campanula macrantha alba* and the fine purple *Campanula macrocarpa* with Male Fern or Lady Fern.

In an open, sunny place *Eryngium giganteum* with Sea-kale.

In a section of flower border given to purple flowers *Salvia Sclarea* with *S. virgata*, and purple-leaved Sage at the foot.

CHAPTER VI

THE MAIN HARDY FLOWER BORDER

THE big flower border is about two hundred feet long and fourteen feet wide. It is sheltered from the north by a solid sandstone wall about eleven feet high clothed for the most part with evergreen shrubs—Bay and Laurustinus, Choisya, Cistus and Loquat. These show as a handsome background to the flowering plants. They are in a three-foot-wide border at the foot of the wall; then there is a narrow alley, not seen from the front, but convenient for access to the wall shrubs and for working the back of the border.

As it is impossible to keep any one flower border fully dressed for the whole summer, and as it suits me that it should be at its best in the late summer, there is no attempt to have it full of flowers as early as June. Another region belongs to June; so that at that time the big border has only some incidents of good bloom, though the ground is rapidly covering with the strong patches, most of them from three to five years old, of the later-blooming perennials. But early in the month there are some clumps of the beautiful *Iris Pallida dalmatica* in the regions of grey foliage, and of the splendid blue-purple bloom of *Geranium ibericum platyphyllum*, the best of the large Cranesbills, and the

THE FLOWER BORDER IN LATE SUMMER: YUCCA, HYDRANGEA, SNAPDRAGON, LILIUM AURATUM, AND EARLY ASTERS, WITH GREY FOLIAGE OF CINERARIA MARITIMA, SANTOLINA AND ELYMUS.

*THE CROSS WALK DIVIDING THE FLOWER BORDER: YUCCA, HYDRANGEA,
MEGASEA AND STACHYS.*

slow-growing *Dictamnus Fraxinella* (the white variety),
and Meadowsweets white and pink, Foxgloves and
Canterbury Bells, and to the front some long-established
sheets of *Iberis sempervirens* that have grown right
on to the path. The large Yuccas, *Y. gloriosa* and
Y. recurva, are throwing up their massive spikes, though
it will be July before they actually flower, and the
blooms on some bushes of the great *Euphorbia Wulfenii*,
although they were flowers of May and their almost
yellow colour is turning greener, are still conspicuous
and ornamental. Then the plants in the middle of
the wall, *Choisya ternata* and *Clematis montana* are still
full of white bloom, and the Guelder Rose is hanging
out its great white balls. I like to plant the Guelder
Rose and *Clematis montana* together. Nothing does
better on north or east walls, and it is pleasant to see
the way the Clematis flings its graceful garlands over
and through the stiff branches of the Viburnum.

The more brilliant patches of colour in the big border
in June are of Oriental Poppies intergrouped with
Gypsophila, which will cover their space when they
have died down, and the earlier forms of *Lilium croceum*
of that dark orange colour that almost approaches
scarlet.

During the first week of June any bare spaces of the
border are filled up with half-hardy annuals, and some
of what we are accustomed to call bedding-plants—such
as Geranium, Salvia, Calceolaria, Begonia, Gazania and
Verbena. The half-hardy annuals are African Marigold, deep orange and pale sulphur, pure white single
Petunia, tall Ageratum, tall striped Maize, white

Cosmos, sulphur Sunflower, *Phlox Drummondi*, Nasturtiums, and *Trachelium cœruleum*. Dahlias were planted out in May, and earlier still the Hollyhocks, quite young plants that are to bloom in August and September ; the autumn-planted ones flowering earlier. The ground was well cleared of weeds before these were planted, and, soon after, the whole border had a good mulch of a mixture of half-rotted leaves and old hot-bed stuff. This serves the double purpose of keeping the soil cool and of affording gradual nutriment when water is given.

The planting of the border is designed to show a distinct scheme of colour arrangement. At the two ends there is a groundwork of grey and glaucous foliage —Stachys, Santolina, *Cineraria maritima*, Sea-kale and Lyme-grass, with darker foliage, also of grey quality, of Yucca, *Clematis recta* and Rue. With this, at the near or western end, there are flowers of pure blue, grey-blue, white, palest yellow and palest pink ; each colour partly in distinct masses and partly inter-grouped. The colouring then passes through stronger yellows to orange and red. By the time the middle space of the border is reached the colour is strong and gorgeous, but, as it is in good harmonies, it is never garish. Then the colour strength recedes in an inverse sequence through orange and deep yellow to pale yellow, white and palest pink ; again with blue-grey foliage. But at this, the eastern end, instead of the pure blues we have purples and lilacs.

Looked at from a little way forward, for a wide space

of grass allows this point of view, the whole border can be seen as one picture, the cool colouring at the ends enhancing the brilliant warmth of the middle. Then, passing along the wide path next the border, the value of the colour arrangement is still more strongly felt. Each portion now becomes a picture in itself, and every one is of such a colouring that it best prepares the eye, in accordance with natural law, for what is to follow. Standing for a few moments before the endmost region of grey and blue, and saturating the eye to its utmost capacity with these colours, it passes with extraordinary avidity to the succeeding yellows. These intermingle in a pleasant harmony with the reds and scarlets, blood-reds and clarets, and then lead again to yellows. Now the eye has again become saturated, this time with the rich colouring, and has therefore, by the law of complementary colour, acquired a strong appetite for the greys and purples. These therefore assume an appearance of brilliancy that they would not have had without the preparation provided by their recently received complementary colour.

There are well-known scientific toys illustrating this law. A short word, printed in large red letters, is looked at for half a minute. The eyes are shut and an image of the same word appears, but the lettering is green. Many such experiments may be made in the open garden. The brilliant orange African Marigold has leaves of a rather dull green colour. But look steadily at the flowers for thirty seconds in sunshine and then look at the leaves. The leaves appear to be bright blue !

Even when a flower border is devoted to a special season, as mine is given to the time from mid-July to October, it cannot be kept fully furnished without resorting to various contrivances. One of these is the planting of certain things that will follow in season of bloom and that can be trained to take each other's places. Thus, each plant of *Gypsophila paniculata* when full grown covers a space a good four feet wide. On each side of it, within reasonable distance of the root, I plant Oriental Poppies. These make their leaf and flower growth in early summer when the Gypsophila is still in a young state. The Poppies will have died down by the time the Gypsophila is full grown and has covered them. After this has bloomed the seed-pods turn brown, and though a little of this colouring is not harmful in the autumn border, yet it is not wanted in such large patches. We therefore grow at its foot, or within easy reach, some of the trailing Nasturtiums, and lead them up so that they cover the greater part of the brown seed-spray.

Delphiniums, which are indispensable for July, leave bare stems with quickly yellowing leafage when the flowers are over. We plant behind them the white Everlasting Pea, and again behind that, Clematis Jackmanii. When the Delphiniums are over, the rapidly forming seed-pods are removed, the stems are cut down to just the right height, and the white Peas are trained over them. When the Peas go out of bloom in the middle of August, the Clematis is brought over. It takes some years for these two plants to become established ; in the case of those I am describing the

LAWN

JAPANESE ANEMONES IN A HALF-SHADY BORDER.

LAWN

Pea has been four or five years planted and the Clematis seven. They cannot be hurried; indeed, in my garden it is difficult to get the Clematis to grow at all. But good gardening means patience and dogged determination. There must be many failures and losses, but by always pushing on there will also be the reward of success. Those who do not know are apt to think that hardy flower gardening of the best kind is easy. It is not easy at all. It has taken me half a lifetime merely to find out what is best worth doing, and a good slice out of another half to puzzle out the ways of doing it.

In addition to these three plants that I grow over one another I am now adding a fourth—the September-blooming *Clematis Flammula*. It must not be supposed that they are just lumped one over another so that the under ones have their leafy growths smothered. They are always being watched, and, bit by bit, the earlier growths are removed as soon as their respective plants are better without them.

Then there is the way of pulling down tall plants whose natural growth is upright. At the back of the yellow part of the border are some plants of a form of *Helianthus orgyalis*, trained down, as described later at p. 72. But other plants can be treated in the same way; the tall Rudbeckia Golden Glow, and Dahlias and Michaelmas Daisies. The tall Snapdragons can also be pulled down and made to cover a surprising space of bare ground with flowering side-shoots.

As it is still impossible to prevent the occurrence of a blank here and there, or as the scene, viewed as a picture, may want some special accentuation or colouring, there is the way of keeping a reserve of plants in pots and dropping them in where they may be wanted. The thing that matters is that, in its season, the border shall be kept full and beautiful; by what means does not matter in the least. For this sort of work some of the most useful plants are Hydrangeas, *Lilium longiflorum, candidum* and *auratum,* and *Campanula pyramidalis,* both white and blue, and, for foliage, *Funkia grandiflora, F. Sieboldi* and hardy Ferns.

An important matter is that of staking and supporting. The rule, as I venture to lay it down, is that sticks and stakes must never show. They must be so arranged that they give the needful support, while allowing the plant its natural freedom; but they must remain invisible. The only time when they are tolerated is for the week or two when they have been put in for Dahlias, when the plants have not yet grown up to cover them.

Michaelmas Daisies we stake with great care in June, putting in some stiff branching spray of oak or chestnut among the growths and under their fronts. At the end of June we also nip the tops of some of the forward growths of the plants so as to vary the outline.

There are two borders of Michaelmas Daisies, one for the earlier sorts that flower in September and the other for the October kinds. They are in places that need not often be visited except in the blooming season, therefore we allow the supporting spray to be seen while the plants are growing. But early in August

GOOD STAKING—CAMPANULA PERSICIFOLIA.

CAREFUL STAKING—THE LATER MICHAELMAS DAISIES.

in the case of the September border, and early in September in the case of the one for October, we go round and regulate the plants, settling them among the sticks in their definite positions. When this is done every atom of projecting spray is cut away with the *sécateur*.

I hold that nothing unsightly should be seen in the garden. The shed for sticks and stakes is a lean-to at one end of the barn, showing to the garden. The roof had to be made at a very low pitch, and there was no roofing material suitable but galvanised iron. But a depth of four inches of peaty earth was put over the iron, and now it is a garden of Stonecrops and other plants that flourish in shallow soil in a hot exposure.

To prevent undue disappointment, those who wish for beautiful flower borders and whose enthusiasm is greater than their knowledge, should be reminded that if a border is to be planted for pictorial effect, it is impossible to maintain that effect and to have the space well filled for any period longer than three months, and that even for such a time there will have to be contrivances such as have been described.

It should also be borne in mind that a good hardy flower border cannot be made all at once. Many of the most indispensable perennials take two, three or even more years to come to their strength and beauty. The best way is to plant the border by a definite plan, allowing due space for the development of each plant. Then, for the first year or two, a greater number of half-hardy annuals and biennials than will eventually be needed should be used to fill the spaces that have not yet been taken up by the permanent plants. The best of these are Pentstemons and Snapdragons, the Snapdragons grown both as annuals and biennials, for so an extended season of bloom is secured. Then there should be African and French Marigolds, the smaller annual Sunflowers, Zinnias, Plume Celosias, China Asters, Stocks, Foxgloves, Mulleins, Ageratum, Phlox Drummondi and Indian Pinks; also hardy annuals—Lupines of several kinds, *Chrysanthemum coronarium*, the fine pink Mallows, Love-in-a-Mist, Nasturtiums or any others that are liked.

CHAPTER VII

THE FLOWER BORDER IN JULY

TOWARDS the end of July the large flower border begins to show its scheme. Until then, although it has been well filled with growing plants, there has been no attempt to show its whole intention. But now this is becoming apparent. The two ends, as already described, are of grey foliage, with, at the near end, flowers of pale blue, white and lightest yellow. The tall spikes of pale blue Delphinium are over, and now there are the graceful grey-blue flowers of *Campanula lactiflora* that stand just in front of the great Larkspurs. At the back is a white Everlasting Pea, four years planted and now growing tall and strong. The over-blown flowers of the Delphinium have been removed, but their stems have been left just the right height for supporting the growth of the white Pea, which is now trained over them and comes forward to meet the pale blue-white Campanula. In front of this there is a drift of Rue, giving a beautiful effect of dim grey colour and softened shadow ; it is crowned by its spreading corymbs of pale yellow bloom that all rise nearly to a level. Again in front is the grand glaucous foliage of Sea-kale. A little further along, and towards the back, is a bush of Golden Privet, taking up and continuing the pale yellow of the Rue blossom, and forming a kind of groundwork to a group of the fine Mullein *Verbascum phlomoides* now fully out. Just below this is a clump of the Double Meadowsweet, a mass of warm white flower-foam. Intergrouped are tall Snapdragons, white and palest yellow. Then forward are the pale blue-green sword-blades of *Iris Pallida dalmatica* that flowered in June. This is one of the few Irises admitted to the border, but it is here because it has the quality, rare among its kind, of maintaining its great leaves in beauty to near the end of the year. Quite to the front are lower-growing plants of purest blue—the Cape Daisy (*Agathea cœlestis*) and blue Lobelia.

Now we pass to a rather large group of *Eryngium oliverianum*, the fine kind that is commonly but wrongly called *E. amethystinum*. It is a deep-rooting perennial that takes three to four years to become strongly established. In front of this are some pale and darker blue Spiderworts (*Tradescantia virginica*), showing best in cloudy weather. At the back is *Thalictrum flavum*, whose bloom is a little overpast, though it still shows some of its foamy-feathery pale yellow. Next we come to stronger yellows, with a middle mass of a good home-grown form of *Coreopsis lanceolata*. This is fronted by a stretch of *Helenium pumilum*. Behind the Coreopsis are *Achillea Eupatorium* and yellow Cannas.

Now the colour strengthens with the Scarlet Balm or Bergamot, intergrouped with *Senecio artemisiæfolius*, a plant little known but excellent in the flower

border. A few belated Orange Lilies have their colour
nearly repeated by the Gazanias next to the path.
The strong colour is now carried on by *Lychnis chalce-
donica*, scarlet Salvia, *Lychnis haageana* (a fine plant
that is much neglected), and some of the dwarf Tropæ-
olums of brightest scarlet. After this we gradually
return to the grey-blues, whites and pale yellows,
with another large patch of *Eryngium oliverianum*,
white Everlasting Pea, Calceolaria, and the splendid
leaf-mass of a wide and high plant of *Euphorbia
Wulfenii*, which, with the accompanying Yuccas, rises
to a height far above my head. Passing between a
clump of Yuccas on either side is the cross-walk
leading by an arched gateway through the wall. The
border beyond this is a shorter length, and has a whole
ground of grey foliage—Stachys, Santolina, Elymus,
Cineraria maritima, and Sea-kale. Then another
group of Rue, with grey-blue foliage and pale yellow
bloom, shows near the extreme end against the full
green of the young summer foliage of the Yew arbour
that comes at the end of the border. Again at this
end is the tall *Campanula lactiflora*. In the nearer
middle a large mass of purple Clematis is trained
over stiff, branching spray, and is beginning to show
its splendid colour, while behind, and looking their
best in the subdued light of the cloudy morning on
which these notes are written, are some plants of
Verbascum phlomoides, ten feet high, showing a great
cloud of pure pale yellow. They owe their vigour
to being self-sown seedlings, never transplanted.
Instead of having merely a blooming spike, as is the

usual way of those that are planted, these have abundant side branches. They dislike bright sunshine, only expanding fully in shade or when the day is cloudy and inclined to be rainy. Close to them, rising to the wall's whole eleven feet of height, is a *Cistus cyprius*, bearing a quantity of large white bloom with a deep red spot at the base of each petal.

Though there is as yet but little bloom in this end of the border, the picture is complete and satisfying. Each one of the few flower-groups tells to the utmost, while the intervening masses of leafage are in themselves beautiful and have the effect of being relatively well disposed. There is also such rich promise of flower beauty to come that the mind is filled with glad anticipation, besides feeling content for the time being with what it has before it. There is one item of colouring that strikes the trained eye as specially delightful. It is a bushy mass of *Clematis recta*, now out of bloom. It occurs between the overhanging purple Clematis and the nearer groups of *Cineraria maritima* and Santolina. The leaves are much deeper in tone than these and have a leaden sort of blueness, but the colouring, both of the parts in light and even more of the mysterious shadows, is in the highest degree satisfactory and makes me long for the appreciative presence of those few friends who are artists both on canvas and in their gardens, and most of all for that of one who is now dead * but to whom I owe, with deepest thankfulness, a precious memory of forty years of helpful and sympathetic guidance and

* The late H. B. Brabazon.

WHITE ROSE LA GUIRLANDE: GREY BORDERS BEYOND.

CLEMATIS RECTA.

encouragement in the observation and study of colour beauty.

One cannot write of the garden in July without a word on the Roses. Besides the bushy garden Roses, and the kinds of special charm, such as Damask, Provence, Moss and China, those that most nearly concern the garden for beauty and pictorial effect are the rambling and climbing Roses that flower in clusters.

In " Roses for English Gardens " I dealt at some length with the many ways of using them ; here I must only touch upon one or two of these ways. But I wish to remind my readers of the great value of these free Roses for running up through such trees as Yews or Hollies in regions where garden joins hands with woodland, and also of their great usefulness for forming lines of arch and garland as an enclosure to some definite space. I have them like this forming the boundary on two sides of a garden of long beds, whose other two sides are a seven-foot wall and the back of a stable and loft. Just beyond the arch in the picture (p. 64), and dividing the little garden in two, is the short piece of double border that is devoted to August.

The other long beds in this region are for special combinations, some of them of July flowers ; *e.g.*, Orange Lilies with the beautiful *Clematis recta*, a plant but little known, though it is easy to grow and is one of the best of summer flowers. One bed is for blue colouring with grey foliage. Here is the lovely

Delphinium Belladonna, with flowers of a blue purer
than that of any other of its beautiful kind. It never
grows tall, nor has it the strong, robust aspect of
the larger ones, but what it lacks in vigour is more
than made up for by the charming refinement of the
whole plant. In the same bed are the other pure blues
of the rare double Siberian Larkspur, and the single
allied kind *Delphinium grandiflorum*, of *Salvia patens*
and of the Cape Daisy (*Agathea cœlestis*). Between the
clumps of Belladonna are bushes of white Lavender,
and the whole is carpeted and edged with the white
foliage of *Artemisia stelleriana*, the quite hardy plant
that is such a good substitute for the tenderer
Cineraria maritima.

Among the best flowers of July that have a place
in this garden are the Pentstemons planted last year.
We grow them afresh from cuttings every autumn,
planting them out in April. They are not quite hardy,
and a bad winter may destroy all the last year's plants.
But if these can be saved they bloom in July, whereas
those planted in the spring of the year do not flower
till later. So we protect the older plants with fir-
boughs and generally succeed in saving them. Old
plants of Snapdragon are also now in flower. They
too are a little tender in the open, although they
are safe in dry-walling with the roots out of the way
of frost and the crowns kept dry among the stones.

Much use is made of a dwarf kind of Lavender that
is also among the best of the July flowers The whole
size of the plant is about cne-third that of the ordinary
kind ; the flowers are darker in colour and the time

DELPHINIUM BELLADONNA.

CANTERBURY BELLS.

of blooming a good month earlier.   It has a different
use in gardening, as the flowers, being more crowded
and of a deeper tint, make a distinct colour effect.
Besides its border use, it is a plant for dry banks, tops
of rock-work and dry-walling.

CHAPTER VIII

THE FLOWER BORDER IN AUGUST

By the second week of August the large flower border is coming to its best. The western grey end, with its main planting of hoary and glaucous foliage—Yucca, Sea-kale, *Cineraria maritima*, Rue, Elymus, Santolina, Stachys, &c.—now has *Yucca flaccida* in flower. This neat, small Yucca, one of the varieties or near relatives of *filamentosa*, is a grand plant for late summer. A well-established clump throws up a quantity of flower-spikes of that highly ornamental character that makes the best of these fine plants so valuable. White Everlasting Pea, planted about three feet from the back, is trained on stout pea-sticks over the space occupied earlier by the Delphiniums and the Spiræas. A little of it runs into a bush of Golden Privet. This Golden Privet is one of the few shrubs that have a place in the flower border. Its clean, cheerful, bright yellow gives a note of just the right colour all through the summer. It has also a solidity of aspect that enhances by contrast the graceful lines of the foliage of a clump of the great Japanese striped grass *Eulalia*, which stands within a few feet of it, seven feet high, shooting upright, but with the ends of the leaves recurved.

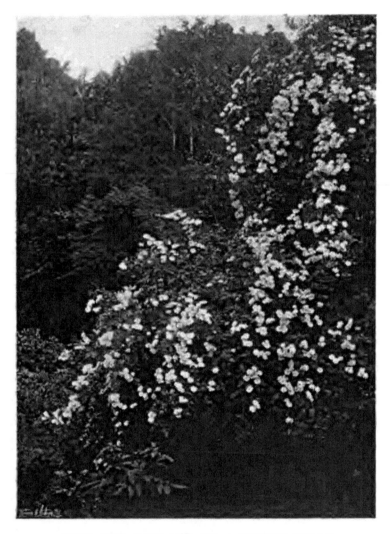

ROSE THE GARLAND IN A SILVER HOLLY.

ERYNGIUM OLIVERIANUM.

Snapdragons, tall white and tall yellow, spire up five feet high, following the earlier Foxgloves. At the back is the pretty pink Dahlia Asia with sulphur and pale pink Hollyhocks. A little further along, and staked out so as to take the place of the clumps of *Verbascum Chaixii* that were so fine at the end of June, is Dahlia Mrs. Hawkins—palest yellow with a slight pink flush. Forward is a group of a Pentstemon of palest pink colouring named Spitzberg, that 1 had from Messrs. Barr's nursery, then a patch or two of palest blue Spiderwort, and, quite to the front; in any spaces there may be among the grey foliage, Lobelia " Cobalt Blue," the taller *Lobelia tenuior*, and the pretty little blue-flowered Cape Daisy, *Agathea cælestis*.

The whole border is backed by a stone wall eleven feet high, now fully clothed with shrubs and plants that take their place in the colour scheme, either for tint of bloom or mass of foliage. Thus the red-leaved Claret Vine shows as background to the rich red region, and *Robinia hispida* stands where its pink clusters will tell rightly ; Choisya and *Cistus cyprius* where their dark foliage and white bloom will be of value ; the greyish foliage and abundant pale lilac blossom of *Abutilon vitifolium* in the grey and purple region, and the pale green foliage of the deciduous *Magnolia conspicua* showing as a background to the tender blue of a charming pale Delphinium.

The shrubs and plants on the wall are not all there because they are things rare and precious or absolutely needing the shelter of the wall, though some of them are glad of it ; but because they give a background that either harmonises in detail with what is in front or will help to enrich or give general cohesion to the picture. The front of the border has some important foliage giving a distinctly blue effect ; prominent among it Sea-kale. The flower-stems are cut hard back in the earlier summer, and it is now in handsome fresh leaf. Further back is the fine blue foliage of Lyme-grass (*Elymus arenarius*), a plant of our sea-shores, but of much value for blue effects in the garden.

Now is the time to begin to use our reserve of plants in pots. Of these the most useful are the Hydrangeas. They are dropped into any vacant spaces, more or less in groups, in the two ends of the border where there is grey foliage, their pale pink colouring agreeing with these places. Their own leafage is a rather bright green, but we get them so well bloomed that but few leaves are seen, and we arrange as cleverly as we can that the rest shall be more or less hidden by the surrounding bluish foliage. I stand a few paces off, directing the formation of the groups ; considering their shape in relation to the border as a whole. I say to the gardener that I want a Hydrangea in such a place, and tell him to find the nearest place where it can be dropped in. Sometimes this dropping in, for the pots have to be partly sunk, comes in the way of some established plant. If it is a deep-rooted perennial that takes three or four years to come to its strength, like an Eryngium or a Dictamnus, of course I avoid encroaching on its root-room. But if

LYME-GRASS AND SANTOLINA.

*TALL CAMPANULAS PYRAMIDALIS AND LACTIFLORA
IN A GREY BORDER.*

it is a thing that blooms the season after it is planted, and of which I have plenty in reserve, such as an Anthemis, a Tradescantia, or a Helenium, I sacrifice a portion of the plant-group, knowing that it can easily be replaced. But then by August many of the plants have spread widely above and there is space below. *Lilium longiflorum* in pots is used in the same way, and for the most part in this blue end of the border, though there are also some at the further, purple end, and just a flash of their white beauty in the middle region of strong reds.

In order to use both blue and purple in the flower border, this cool, western, grey-foliaged end has the blues, and the further, eastern end the purples. For although I like to use colour as a general rule in harmonies rather than contrasts, I prefer to avoid, except in occasional details, a mixture of blue and purple. At this end, therefore, there are flowers of pure blue —Delphinium, Anchusa, Salvia, Blue Cape Daisy and Lobelia, and it is only when the main mass of blue, of Delphiniums and Anchusas, is over that even the presence of the pale grey-blue of *Campanula lactiflora* is made welcome. Near the front is another pale grey-blue, that of *Clematis davidiana*, just showing a few blooms, but not yet fully out.

Now, giving a pleasant rest and refreshment to the eye after the blues and greys, is a well-shaped drift of the pale sulphur African Marigold. It was meant to be the dwarf variety, but, as it grows two and a half feet high, it has been pulled down as it grew. Some of it has been brought down some way over the edge of the path, where it breaks the general front line pleasantly and shows off its good soft colouring. We grow only this pale colour and a good form of the splendid orange. The intermediate one, the full yellow African Marigold, has, to my eye, a raw quality that I am glad to avoid, and I have other plants that give the strong yellow colour better. Now at the back are some plants of the single Hollyhock, *Hibiscus ficifolius*, white and pale yellow, recalling, as we merge into the stronger yellows, the colouring of the region just left. They are partly intergrouped with that excellent plant Rudbeckia Golden Glow, brilliant, long-lasting, and capable of varied kinds of useful treatment.

Now we come to a group of the perennial Sunflowers ; a good form of the double *Helianthus multiflorus* in front, and behind it the large single kind of the same plant. By the side of these is a rather large group of a garden form of *H. orgyalis*. This is one of the perennial Sunflowers that are usually considered not good enough for careful gardening. It grows very tall, and bears a smallish bunch of yellow flowers at the top. If this were all it could do, it would not be in my flower border. But in front of it grows a patch of the fine Tansy-like *Achillea Eupatorium*, and in front of this again a wide-spreading group of *Eryngium oliverianum*—beautiful all through July. When the bloom of these is done the tall Sunflower is trained down over them—this pulling down, as in the case of so many plants, causing it to throw up flower-stalks from the axils of every pair of leaves ; so that in

September the whole thing is a sheet of bloom. Thus the plant that was hardly worth a place in the border becomes, at its flowering time, one of the brightest ornaments of the garden. Other plants that are in front of the Sunflower, that have also passed out of bloom, are the Scarlet Bee-balm (*Monarda*) and the very useful alpine Groundsel (*Senecio artemisiæfolius*).

Next we have an important group of a large-leaved Canna, the handsomest foliage in the border; good to see when the sun is behind and the light comes through the leaves. Here also, at the back, is a patch of Hollyhocks—one very dark, almost a claret-red, and a fine, full red inclining to blood-colour. They tower up together, and close to them are Dahlias, the rich red Lady Ardilaun, deep scarlet Cochineal, bright scarlet Fire King, and its variety Orange Fire King, now the most brilliant piece of colouring in the garden. These lead on to a gorgeous company—Phlox Coquelicot, scarlet Pentstemon, orange African Marigold, scarlet Gladiolus, and, to the front, a brilliant dwarf scarlet Salvia; *Helenium pumilum* and scarlet and orange dwarf Nasturtium. Here and there within this mass of bright colouring there is a patch of the fine deep yellow *Coreopsis lanceolata*, a plant of long-enduring bloom, or rather of long succession, for, if the dead flowers are removed, it will look bright for a good three months.

As this gorgeous mass occupies a large space in the flower border, I have thought well to subdue it here and there with the cloudy masses of *Gypsophila paniculata* Five-year-old plants of this form masses

of the pretty mist-like bloom four feet across and as
much high. This bold introduction of grey among
the colour masses has considerable pictorial value.
As the grey changes, towards the end of the
month, to a brownish tone, some of the tall Nasturtiums are allowed to grow over the bushes of
Gypsophila.

Now we have got beyond the middle of the length
of the border, and the colour changes again to the
clear and pale yellows, and then again to the grey
foliage as at the beginning. Where this occurs, at a
little more than two-thirds of the way along the border,
it is crossed by the path, leading, through an archway
in the wall closed by a door, to the garden beyond.
This cross-path is flanked by groups of Yuccas, slightly
raised, as will be seen in some of the illustrations. (*See*
pp. 53, 112.) Yuccas all like a raised mound and some
good loam to grow in. I have them here as well as
at the two extreme ends of the border. No plants
make a handsomer full-stop to any definite garden
scheme. The grey treatment comprises the two
Yucca mounds to right and left of the cross-path ;
the other grey plants are as before—*Cineraria maritima*, Santolina, Stachys, Elymus and Rue—but at
this end, besides some plants with white, pink and
palest yellow colouring, the other flowers are not blues,
but purples, light and dark. Among these a very
useful thing is Ageratum ; not the dwarf Ageratum,
though this is good too in its place, but the ordinary
Ageratum mexicanum, a plant that grows about two
feet high. This is also the place for some of the earliest

YUCCA FILAMENTOSA VAR. FLACCIDA.

THE GREY BORDERS: STACHYS, GYPSOPHILA, LILY, ACHILLEA PEARL AND PINK HOLLYHOCK.

Michaelmas Daisies that will bloom in September, such as *Aster acris* and *A. Shortii*. At the back there are Dahlias, white and pale yellow, with white and sulphur Hollyhocks, and, in the middle spaces, pale pink Gladiolus, double *Saponaria officinalis*, and pale pink Pentstemon. At the back, also, there is a clump of Globe Thistle (*Echinops*) and a grand growth of Clematis Jackmanii, following in season of bloom, and partly led over, a white Everlasting Pea, that in the earlier summer was trained to conceal the dying stems of the red-orange Lilies that bloomed in June.

There is also a short length of double border specially devoted to August, of the same character, though not so fully developed, as what will be described in a further chapter as the Grey Garden. Here, the space being small, it has been given specially to the more restricted season. The scheme of colouring has a ground of grey foliage, with flowers of pink, white, and light and dark purple.

Next the path is the silvery white of Stachys, *Cineraria maritima* and *Artemisia stelleriana*, with the grey foliage and faint purple of the second bloom of Catmint. Then bushy masses of Lavender and Gypsophila, and between them *Lilium longiflorum*, Godetia Double Rose and white Snapdragons. Behind and among these are groups of the clear white Achillea The Pearl, and the round purple heads of Globe-thistle. Here and there, pushing to the front, is a Silver Thistle (*Eryngium giganteum*). At the back shoot up Pink

Hollyhocks, the kind being one of home growth known as Pink Beauty. The deep green of a Fig-tree that covers the upper part of the landing and outside stone steps to a loft, is an excellent background to the tender greys of these August borders. Unfortunately, the main group of pink Hollyhock, that should have stood up straight and tall and shown well against the window and silvery-grey weather-boarding of the loft, failed altogether last season ; in fact, all the Holly-hocks were poor and stunted, so that an important part of the intended effect was lost.

Of Lavender hedges there are several, of varying ages, in different parts of the garden. Lavender for cutting should be from plants not more than four to five years old, but for pictorial effect the bushes may be much older. When they are growing old it is a good plan to plant white and purple Clematises so that they can be trained freely through and over them.

There are comparatively few shrubs that flower in autumn, so that it is quite a pleasant surprise to come upon a group of them all in bloom together. The picture shows the satisfactory effect of a group of *Æsculus parviflora* and *Olearia Haastii*. It would have been all the better for some plants of the beau-tiful blue-flowered *Perowskya atriplicifolia* and for *Caryopteris mastacanthus* in front, but at the time of planting I did not think of the *Caryopteris* and did not know the *Perowskya*. (See p. 77.)

August is the month of China Asters. I find many

A LAVENDER HEDGE,

ÆSCULUS PARVIFLORA AND OLEARIA HAASTII.

people are shy of these capital plants, perhaps because
the mixtures, such as are commonly grown, contain
rather harsh and discordant colours; also perhaps
because a good many of the kinds, having been pur-
posely dwarfed in order to fit them for pot-culture
and bedding, are too stiff to look pretty in general
gardening. Such kinds will always have their uses,
but what is wanted now in the best gardening is
more freedom of habit. I have a little space that
I give entirely to China Asters. I have often had
the pleasure of showing it to some person who pro-
fessed a dislike to them, and with great satisfaction
have heard them say, with true admiration: "Oh!
but I had no idea that China Asters could be so
beautiful."

It is only a question of selection, for the kinds are
now so many and the colourings so various that there
are China Asters to suit all tastes and uses. My own
liking is for those of the pure violet-purple and lavender
colours, with whites; and to plants with these clear,
clean tints my Aster garden is restricted. In other
places I grow some of the tenderer pinks, a good blood-
red and a clear pale yellow; but these are kept quite
away from the purples. The kinds chosen are within
the Giant Comet, Ostrich Plume and Victoria classes—
all plants with long-stalked bloom and a rather free
habit of growth. For some years I was much hindered
from getting the colours I wanted from the inaccurate
way in which they are described in seed-lists. Finally
I paid a visit to the trial-grounds of one of our premier
seed-houses, and saw all the kinds and the colourings

and made my own notes. I cannot but think that a
correct description of the colours, instead of a fanciful
one, would help both customer and seed-merchant.
As it is, the customer, in order to get the desired flowers,
has to *learn a code*. I have often observed, in com-
paring French and English seed-lists, that the French
do their best to describe colours accurately, but that
the English use some wording which does not describe
the colour, but appears to be intended as a compli-
mentary euphemism. Thus, if I want a Giant Comet
of that beautiful pale silvery lavender, perhaps the
loveliest colour of which a China Aster is capable, I
have to ask for " azure blue." If I want a full lilac,
I must order " blue "; if a full purple, it is " dark
blue." If I want a strong, rich violet-purple, I must
beware of asking for purple, for I shall get a terrible
·magenta such as one year spoilt the whole colour
scheme of my Aster garden. It is not as if the right
colour-words were wanting, for the language is rich
in them—violet, lavender, lilac, mauve, purple :
these, with slight additions, will serve to describe
the whole of the colourings falsely called blue.
The word blue should not be used at all in connection with these flowers. There are no blue China
Asters.

The diagram shows a simple arrangement for a
little garden of China Asters of the purple and white
colourings. The seed-list names are used in order
to identify the sorts recommended. A Lavender
hedge surrounds the whole ; the paths are edged with
Stachys lanata. Taking Messrs. Sutton's list and

PLAN OF A SMALL GARDEN OF CHINA ASTERS

translating into colour-words as usually understood, the tints are :

Seed list name	Actual colour
Azure-blue	Tender pale lavender-lilac.
Blue	Light purple.
Dark blue	Rich dark purple.

I had hoped that Messrs. Sutton had in contemplation a revision of some of these puzzling colour-names, but have not, as yet, seen any such desirable alteration.

CHAPTER IX

BEDDING PLANTS

THIS is a conveniently comprehensive term for the tender plants that are put out for the summer. To these plants a small portion of my garden, well sheltered within enclosing walls and yet open to full sunshine, is devoted, so that the little place is in some kind of beauty from the end of July to the last days of September. There has been so strong a revulsion in garden practice since the days when the bedding out of tender plants in stiff and not very intelligent ways absorbed the entire horticultural energy of owners of gardens that many people have conceived a dislike to the plants themselves. It is a common thing for friends to express surprise at seeing scarlet Geraniums, yellow Calceolaria and blue Lobelia in my garden, forgetting that it was not the fault of the plants that they were misused or employed in dull or even stupid ways. There are no better summer flowers than the single and double zonal Pelargoniums that we commonly call Geraniums, and none so good for such uses as the filling of tubs and vases; for not only do they enjoy full sunlight, but they benefit by the extra warmth at the root that they obtain by being raised in the warm air above the ground level. There certainly are among these good summer flowers, a few kinds of harsh, unpleasant reds and pinks, but these are easily avoided, and the range of good colouring, from purest scarlet, through softer tones, to tints of salmon and tender warm pink, is now so great that there is no difficulty in obtaining any combination or sequence that may be desired, such as the very simple one that is shown in the plan and will presently be described.

The little garden is an odd-shaped piece of ground, roughly triangular. The main clump is more than thirty feet wide at one end, a width too great to treat conveniently. It has therefore been arranged with a kind of elevated backbone, a few feet wide, raised less than two feet above the level, with dry walling on each side to retain the earth. As it approaches the narrow end of the triangle it swings round symmetrically on each side forward to the path. All this raised part is treated quite differently to the rest of the garden. There is no attempt at brilliant colouring, but rather to have important masses of fine form in a quiet range of greyish tinting that shall serve as a suitable background to the brighter effects. The planting is mainly of Yuccas of both large and small kinds and of two kinds of Euphorbia ; the bold and striking *E. Wulfenii* with its handsome form of leaf-mass and immense bloom, and the smaller *E. Characias*. Where the walls come near the path there are hanging sheets of the bluish grey foliage of *Othonnopsis cheirifolia*. As will be seen by the plan, the raised mass is fairly wide at the south-western end. Spaces next the path are filled with flowers of pink and purple colouring

such as Heliotrope, Ivy Geranium Mme. Crousse and
Verbena Miss Willmott. The star-shaped figures on
the plan show the Yuccas; the larger ones are *Y.
gloriosa* and *Y. recurva*, and the smaller, garden
varieties of *Y. filamentosa*. There is always a good
proportion of these Yuccas in bloom during the late
summer, so that, standing at the north-west corner,
the stately flower spikes have a fine effect rising above
the colour masses of the borders on the lower level.

These are in two main connected colour schemes—
in gradations of reds, and of whites and yellows re-
spectively. In the red portions the front is chiefly of
Geraniums; Paul Crampel for the strongest red; it is
a little softer and more pleasing to me than Raspail,
which we formerly used. My eye has had too much
tender tutoring to endure the popular Henry Jacoby—
a colour that, for all its violence, has a harsh dullness
that I find displeasing. Next to Paul Crampel we put
one of the softer reds such as Mrs. Bartleman, and this
leads to the fine salmon-coloured King of Denmark,
and then to the paler salmon pink of Mme. Lemoine, a
plant that has the additional advantage of a beautifully
zoned leaf. Some such arrangement is followed
throughout those portions of the garden where red
colouring prevails; the plants for the back being three
varieties of red-bloomed Cannas, one of them with well-
coloured red foliage, and a larger growing kind with
great leaves so much like those of a Banana that,
having lost its original name, we know it as Canna Musa.
This has the leaves slightly red-tinted. With these
Cannas, arranged as shown in the plan, are thin drifts

THE GARDEN OF SUMMER FLOWERS

of Gladiolus Brenchleyensis and others of near colouring, among them the very fine and free Gladiolus Childsii William Faulkner; also the best of the scarlet and orange-scarlet Dahlias, both of the larger-flowered and pompon kinds, scarlet Pentstemon, Alonsoa, Lobelia cardinalis, and, behind the Geraniums, Salvia Pride of Zurich. In several places among the reds comes a drift of a fine garden form of the native *Sedum Telephium*. The quiet grey-green of the plant turns to a subdued chocolate-red, as the large, flat flower-head is developed. The introduction of this undergrowth of quieter related colouring greatly enhances the quality of the livelier reds and helps to put the whole thing together. One break of a white Lily (*L. longiflorum*) comes with fine effect among the reds.

The yellow and white portions pass from the palest of the Geraniums with a front planting of the useful, but in the past much misused, Golden Feather Feverfew, and a rather large quantity of a capital old garden plant, that has of late been much neglected, the variegated form of a native plant *Mentha rotundifolia*. The Feverfew is allowed to flower, but the variegated Mint has the flowering branches cut back so as to keep it to a more convenient height. It is one of the prettiest things as an underplanting to anything of white or yellow colour, and specially charming among the white Lilies (*L. longiflorum*); here and there it is brightened with thin drifts of the pale canary-yellow *Calceolaria amplexicaulis*. The plan shows the general arrangement of the other white and yellow flowers; yellow-bloomed Cannas both tall and short, Snapdragons white, lemon-white and yellow, and Primrose African Marigold. It needs some care to obtain the right colour of this Marigold. There are three distinct colourings of this fine half-hardy annual—the well-known deep orange, a middle yellow and the primrose. Unless the primrose or sulphur colour is insisted on seedsmen are apt to send the middle colour. I have it always from Messrs. Barr and Sons, who send the right colour without fail.

The little garden has a rather high wall to the south, covered with climbing plants and shrubs treated as wall plants. On the northern side an earth bank four and a half feet high, dry-walled on both sides, has the top planted with bushy things. At the western end a fruiting Barberry is thickly overgrown with the large-flowered white Jasmine; then come other shrubby plants, with bush and Rambling Roses and Scotch Briars; the whole forming a flowery fence nearly as high as the opposite wall and affording comforting shelter. It is thickened by having a number of bushes of Choisya in a narrow border on the south side that have grown up to the height of the shrubs in the wall top.

SOME OF THE EARLY ASTERS.

THE SEPTEMBER GARDEN.

CHAPTER X

THE FLOWER BORDERS IN SEPTEMBER

THE main flower border shows in September much the same aspect as in August. But early in the month the middle mass of strong colouring, enhanced by Tritomas and the fuller bloom of Dahlias, is at its brightest. The bold masses of Canna foliage have also grown up and show their intended effect. They form one of the highest points in the border. No attempt is made to keep all the back-row plants standing high ; on the contrary, many that would be the tallest are pulled down to do colour work of medium height. The effect is much more pictorial when the plants at the back rise only here and there to a height of nine or ten feet ; mounting gradually and by no means at equal distances, but somewhat as the forms of greater altitude rise in the ridge of a mountain range. The diagram shows how it comes in the case of my own border in September. (*See* p. 57.)

Rather near the front, the bushy masses of Gypso-phila, which a month ago were silvery grey, have now turned to a brownish colour. They are partly covered with trailing Nasturtiums, but the portions of brown cloud that remain tone well with the rich reds that are near them. In the back of this region dark claret and

blood-red Hollyhocks still show colour, and scarlet
Dahlias are a mass of gorgeous bloom. Their nearest
neighbours are tall flaming Tritomas, with, in front of
them, one of the dwarfer Tritomas that is crowded with
its orange-scarlet flowers of a rather softer tone. Then
come scarlet Gladiolus, a wide group of a splendid red
Pentstemon, and, to the front, an edging and partly
carpeting mass of the good, short-growing form of *Salvia
splendens* called Pride of Zurich.

After these strong reds comes a drift of the brilliant
orange African Marigold, one of the most telling
plants of the time of year. Coming to the yellows of
middle strength, there are some of the perennial Sunflowers, among them the one that seems to be a form of
Helianthus orgyalis, described in the last chapter. This
and some others are trained down to cover plants
now out of bloom. The fine double Rudbeckia called
Golden Glow is treated in the same way. Intergrouped
with it is a useful pale form of *Helianthus lætiflorus*
that takes up the colour when the Rudbeckia is failing.
In the near end region of blue-grey foliage the bloom
of *Clematis davidiana*, also of a greyish blue, but of a
colour quality that is almost exclusively its own, tones
delightfully with its nearest neighbours of leaf and
bloom. About here some pots of · *Plumbago capensis*
are dropped in ; their wide-ranging branches, instead
of being stiffly tied, are trained over some bushy plants
of leaden-blue-foliaged Rue. Near this, and partly
shooting up through some of the same setting, are the
spikes of a beautiful Gladiolus of pale, cool pink colour,
the much-prized gift of an American garden-loving

THE SEPTEMBER GARDEN : LOWER END.

THE SEPTEMBER GARDEN : UPPER END.

friend. Tall white Snapdragons, five feet high, show finely among the gracefully recurved leaves of the blue Lyme-grass. Beyond is a group of *Lilium auratum*, and in the more distant front, pale sulphur African Marigold, just now at its best.

The further end of the border also has grey foliage associated with pink Hydrangeas, white and pink Snapdragons, white Dahlias, purple Clematis, *Lilium auratum* and *Aster acris*. *Yucca flaccida* is still in beauty.

There is another range of double border for the month of September alone. It passes down through the middle of the kitchen garden and is approached by an arch of Laburnum. It is backed on each side by a Hornbeam hedge some five and a half feet high. This border is mainly for the earlier Michaelmas Daisies ; those that bloom in the first three weeks of the month. Grey foliage in plenty is to the front   Running in between the groups is *Artemisia stelleriana*, the quite hardy plant that so well imitates *Cineraria maritima ;* there are also Stachys and White Pink. Further back among the flowers are drifts of the grey-blue Lyme-grass, some grey bushes of Phlomis and a silvery-leaved Willow, kept to a suitable size by careful pruning.

The scheme of colouring consists of this groundwork of grey foliage, with white, lilac, purple and pale pink flowers ; and, breaking into this colouring in two or three distinct places, flowers of pale yellow and yellowish white with suitable accompanying leafage. There is also, in quite another part of the garden, a later border of other Michaelmas Daisies that will follow this in time of blooming. But the September borders have a very different appearance because of their flowers of pink and yellow, colours which are absent in those of the later season.

The yellow flowers are the pale sulphur African Marigold and pale yellow and whitish-yellow tall Snapdragons, with bordering masses of variegated Coltsfoot, and the Golden Feather Feverfew allowed to bloom. The pink colourings are the wide-headed *Sedum spectabile*, pink Japan Anemone and a few pale pink Gladioli. The whites are Dahlias Constance and Henry Patrick, *Pyrethrum uliginosum*, the charming perennial Aster Colerette Blanche and a taller white or yellowish-white Aster with rough stems and harsh-feeling foliage that I know as *A. umbellatus*. Here also are white Japan Anemones, white Snapdragons and white China Asters of the large, long-stemmed, late-blooming kind that were formerly known as Vick's, but are now called Mammoth. Among the grey bordering plants are groups of dwarf Ageratum, one of the best of the tender plants of September and quite excellent with the accompanying grey foliage. The grey bordering is not merely an edging but a general front groundwork, running here and there a yard deep into the border.

Begonias are at their best throughout the month of September. Beds of Begonias alone never seem to me quite satisfactory. Here there is no opportunity for growing them in beds, but I have them in a bit of narrow border that is backed by shrubs that is kept constantly

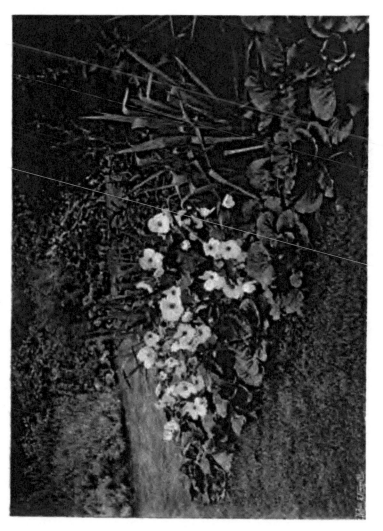

BEGONIAS IN A SETTING OF MEGASEA FOLIAGE.

EARLY ASTERS AND PYRETHRUM ULIGINOSUM.

Upper bed:

Silene (wilica) — C F — A. Munsteal purple — Pyrethrum uliginosum — A. paniculatus — Pyrethrum uliginosum

Arum autumnale — A. acris — A. Colvette Blanche — Phlomis — A. n.B seedling — Anemone Japonica pink

Heliotrope — A. Amellus — white Pink — Sedum spectabile — Stachys

Lower bed:

A. white — Sedum spectabile — Stachys — Artemisia stelleriana — White Pink

purple — A. Amellus — A. n.A Ryecroft purple — A. acris

white — lia & Hollyhock — A. n.A Ryecroft purple — Pyrethrum uliginosum — 2 Phlomis fruticosa — A. puniceus — Pyrethrum — A. Margaret — Euphorbia Charaqas

FEET
0

...AS DAISIES.

enriched. A groundwork of the large-leaved form of *Megasea cordifolia* is planted so as to surround variously sized groups of Begonias—groups of from five to nine plants. The setting of the more solid leaves gives the Begonias a better appearance and makes their bright bloom tell more vividly. They follow in this sequence of colouring : yellow, white, palest pink, full pink, rose, deep red, deep rose, salmon-rose, red-lead colour or orange-scarlet, scarlet, red-lead and orange.

It is a matter of great regret that the best kind of Dahlias for garden effect have lost favour with nurserymen, so that it is now difficult, if not impossible, to obtain from them the most desirable kinds. These are a selection of those that were first called Cactus Dahlias, much more free in form than the old show Dahlias; but with the petals not attenuated and pointed as they are in the modern Cactus kinds. The greater number of these, pretty though their individual blooms are on the show-table, are but of little use in the garden, whereas the old sorts, King of the Cactus, Cochineal, Lady Ardilaun, Fire King and Orange Fire King, are among the most gorgeous of our September flowers. In the same class are : Mrs. Hawkins, palest lemon flushed with pink ; William Pearse, bright yellow ; Lady M. Marsham, bright copper ; J. W. Standling, orange (the two last about four feet high) ; and the two good whites, Constance and Henry Patrick. Of these, all in my opinion indispensable kinds, only Fire King, as far as I am aware, survives in contemporary trade lists.

CHAPTER XI

WOOD AND SHRUBBERY EDGES

OPPORTUNITIES for good gardening are so often over-looked that it may be well to draw attention to some of those that are most commonly neglected.

When woodland joins garden ground there is too often a sudden jolt ; the wood ends with a hard line, sometimes with a path along it, accentuating the defect. When the wood is of Scotch Fir of some age there is a monotonous emptiness of naked trunk and bare ground. In wild moorland this is characteristic and has its own beauty ; it may even pleasantly accompany the garden when there is only a view into it here and there ; but when the path passes along, furlong after furlong, with no attempt to bring the wood into harmony with the garden, then the monotony becomes oppressive and the sudden jolt is unpleasantly perceived. There is the well-stocked garden and there is the hollow wood with no cohesion between the two—no sort of effort to make them join hands.

It would have been better if from the first the garden had not been brought quite so close to the wood, then the space between, anything from twenty-five to forty feet, might have been planted so as to bring them into unison. In such a case the path would go, not next

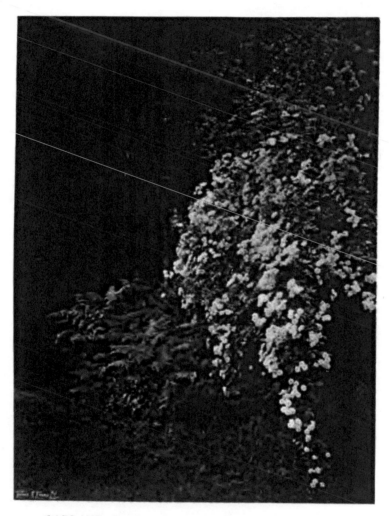

GARLAND ROSE, WHERE GARDEN JOINS WOOD.

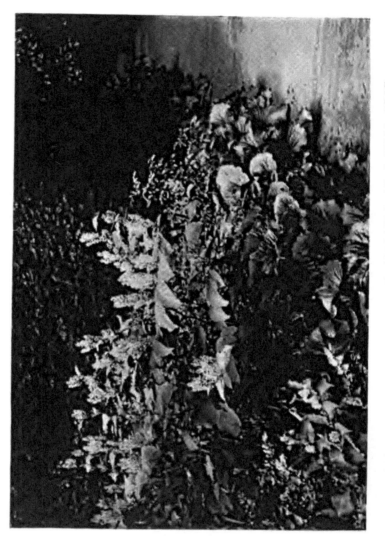

POLYGONUM COMPACTUM AND MEGASEA AT A WOOD EDGE.

the trees, but along the middle of the neutral ground, and would be so planted as to belong equally to garden and wood. The trees would then take their place as the bounding and sheltering feature. It is better to plan it like this at first than to gain the space by felling the outer trees, because the trees at the natural wood edge are better furnished with side branches. Such ground on the shady side of the Scotch Firs would be the best possible site for a Rhododendron walk, and for Azaleas and Kalmias, kept distinct from the Rhododendrons. Then the Scotch Fir indicates the presence of a light peaty soil ; the very thing for that excellent but much-neglected undershrub *Gaultheria Shallon.* This is one of the few things that will grow actually under the Firs, not perhaps in the densest part of an old wood, but anywhere about its edges, or where any light comes in at a clearing or along a cart-way. When once established it spreads with a steady abundance of increase, creeping underground and gradually clothing more and more of the floor of the wood. The flower and fruit have already been shown at pp. 20, 21.

The Great Wood-rush (*Luzula sylvatica*) is also a capital plant for filling bare spaces in wood edges. It does not look like a Rush, but like a broad-leaved Grass. The flowers come in May ; loose, spreading clusters of brownish bloom that rise a good two feet above the tufts of handsome foliage.

Rhododendrons are usually planted much too close together. This is a great mistake ; they should not be nearer than eight to ten feet, or even further, apart, especially in the case of *ponticum* and some of the

larger-growing kinds. It is a common practice to fill
up the edges of their prepared places with a collection
of Heaths. The soil will no doubt suit Heaths, but I
never do it or recommend it because I feel that the
right place for Heaths is quite open ground, and there
are other plants that I think look better with the young
Rhododendrons. For my own liking the best of these
are hardy Ferns—Male Fern, Lady Fern and Dilated
Shield Fern, with groups of Lilies : *L. longiflorum* and
the lovely rosy *L. rubellum* towards the front, and
L. auratum further back. Some of the Andromedas,
especially *Catesbæi* and *axillaris* of the *Leucothoë*
section, are capital plants for this use. Besides Lilies,
a few other flowering plants suitable for the Rhododendron walk are : white Foxgloves, white Columbine,
white *Epilobium angustifolium, Trillium, Epimedium
pinnatum, Uvularia grandiflora, Dentaria diphylla* and
Gentiana asclepiadea. In the same region, and also partly
as edgings to the Rhododendron clumps, suitable small
bushes are *Rhododendron myrtifolium,* the Alpenrose
(*R. ferruginium*) and the sweet-leaved *Ledum palustre.*

Later it was found that these wood-path edges
offered such suitable places for the late-blooming Willow
Gentian (*G. asclepiadea*), that it was still more largely
planted. It delights in a cool place in shade or half-
shade, and when in mid-September so many flowers
are over and garden plants in general are showing
fatigue and exhaustion, it is a pleasure to come upon
the graceful arching sprays, their upper portions set
with pairs of long blue flowers, looking fresh and
bright and full of vigour.

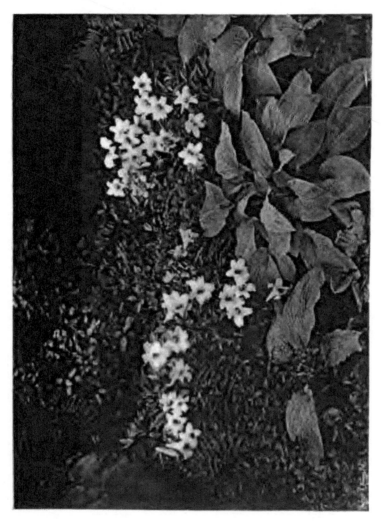

LILIES AND FUNKIAS AT A SHRUBBERY EDGE.

OLEARIA GUNNI, FERN AND FUNKIA AT A SHRUBBERY EDGE.

When the garden comes on the sunny side of the wood the planting would be quite different. Here is the place for Cistuses; for the bolder groups the best are *C. laurifolius* and *C. cyprius*, backed by plantings of Tamarisk, Arbutus and White Broom, with here and there a free-growing Rose of the wilder sort, such as the type *polyantha* and *Brunonis*. If the fir-boughs come down within reach, the wild Clematis (*C. Vitalba*) can be led into them; it will soon ramble up the tree, filling it with its pretty foliage and abundance of August bloom.

The Cistuses delight in a groundwork of Heath; the wild Calluna looks as well as any, but if cultivated kinds are used they should be in good quantities of one sort at a time, and never as hard edgings, but as free carpeting masses.

For the edges of other kinds of woodland the free Roses are always beautiful; where a Holly comes to the front, a Rose such as Dundee Rambler or the Garland will grow up it, supported by its outer branches in the most delightful way. The wild Clematis is in place here too, also the shade-loving plants already named. In deciduous woodland there is probably some undergrowth of Hazel, or of Bramble and wild Honeysuckle. White Foxgloves should be planted at the edge and a little way back, Daffodils for the time when the leaves are not yet there, and Lily of the Valley, whose charming bloom and brilliant foliage come with the young leaves of May.

Where the wood comes nearest the house with only lawn between, it is well to have a grouping of hardy

Ferns and Lilies ; where it is giving place to garden ground and there is a shrubby background, the smaller Polygonums, such as *P. compactum*, are in place.

The spaces more or less wide between large shrubs and turf are full of opportunities for ingenious treatment ; they are just the places most often neglected, or at any rate not well enough considered. I have always taken delight in working out satisfactory ways of treating them. It seems desirable to have, next the grass, some foliage of rather distinct and important size or form. For this use the Megaseas are invaluable, the one most generally useful being the large variety of *M. cordifolia*. Funkias are also beautiful, but as their leaves come late and go with the first frosts or even earlier, whereas the Megaseas persist the whole year round, the latter are the most generally desirable. These shrub-edge spaces occur for the most part in bays, giving an inducement to invent a separate treatment for each bay.

The two illustrations with the front planting of *Funkia Sieboldi* are two adjoining bays ; one showing the charming shrubby Aster *Olearia Gunni* in the middle of June, the other some groups of *Lilium longiflorum*, planted in November of the year before, and in bloom in early August.

Sometimes a single plant of *Gypsophila paniculata* will fill the whole of one of the recesses or bays between the larger shrubs ; *Hydrangea paniculata* is another good filling plant, and the hardy Fuchsias ; both of these, though really woody shrubs, being cut down every winter and treated as herbaceous plants.

FERNS AND LILIES AT A SHRUBBERY EDGE NEXT THE WOOD.

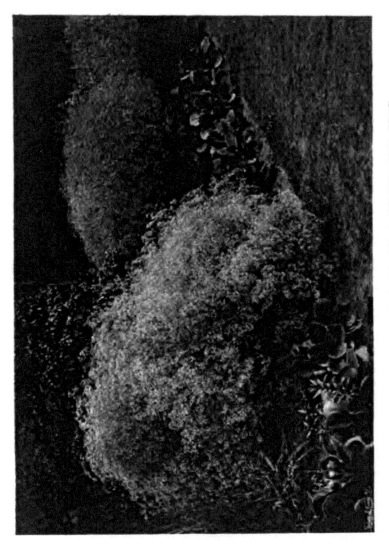

GYPSOPHILA AND MEGASEA AT A SHRUBBERY EDGE.

LILIES AND FERNS AT THE WOOD EDGE NEAR THE LAWN.

ASTER CORYMBOSUS AT SHRUB EDGE. SECOND YEAR AFTER PLANTING.

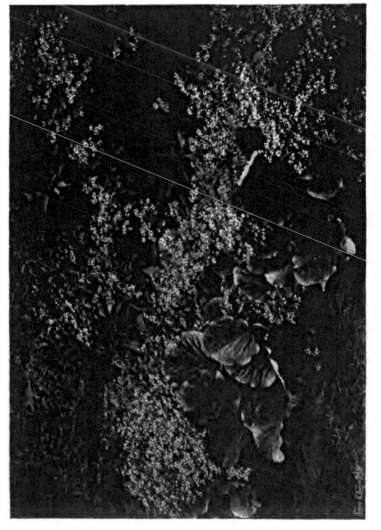

ASTER CORYMBOSUS AT SHRUB EDGE. THIRD YEAR AFTER PLANTING.

STOBÆA PURPUREA, A WALL PLANT FOR A SUNNY PLACE.

There is a small-growing perennial Aster, *A. corymbosus*, from a foot to eighteen inches high, that seems to enjoy close association with other plants and is easy to grow anywhere. I find it, in conjunction with Megasea, one of the most useful of these filling plants for edge spaces that just want some pretty trimming but are not wide enough for anything larger. The same group was photographed two years running. The first year the bloom was a little thicker below, but the second I thought it still better when it had partly rambled up into the lower branches of the Weigela that stood behind it. The little thin starry flower is white and is borne in branching heads ; the leaves are lance-shaped and sharply pointed; but when the plant is examined in the hand its most distinct character is the small fine wire-like stem, smooth and nearly black, that branches about in an angular way of its own.

These are only a very few examples of what may also be done in a number of other ways, but if they serve to draw attention to those generally neglected shrub edges, it may be to the benefit of many gardens. Where there is room for a good group of plants they should be of bold and solid habit, such as Tree Lupine, Peony, Acanthus, *Spiræa Aruncus*, the larger hardy Ferns, *Rubus nutkanus*, or plants of some such size and character. The low-growing *Bambusa tessellata* is a capital shrub-edge plant.

CHAPTER XII

GARDENS OF SPECIAL COLOURING

IT is extremely interesting to work out gardens in which some special colouring predominates, and to those who, by natural endowment or careful eye-cultivation, possess or have acquired what artists understand by an eye for colour, it opens out a whole new range of garden delights.

Arrangements of this kind are sometimes attempted, for occasionally I hear of a garden for blue plants, or a white garden, but I think such ideas are but rarely worked out with the best aims. I have in mind a whole series of gardens of restricted colouring, though I have not, alas, either room or means enough to work them out for myself, and have to be satisfied with an all-too-short length of double border for a grey scheme. But besides my small grey garden I badly want others, and especially a gold garden, a blue garden and a green garden ; though the number of these desires might easily be multiplied.

It is a curious thing that people will sometimes spoil some garden project for the sake of a word. For instance, a blue garden, for beauty's sake, may be hungering for a group of white Lilies, or for something of palest lemon-yellow, but it is not allowed to have it

THE GREY BORDERS: GYPSOPHILA, ECHINOPS, PINK
HOLLYHOCK, HELIOTROPE AND SILVER THISTLE.

OCTOBER BORDERS OF MICHAELMAS DAISIES.

because it is called the blue garden, and there must be no flowers in it but blue flowers. I can see no sense in this; it seems to me like fetters foolishly self-imposed. Surely the business of the blue garden is to be beautiful as well as to be blue. My own idea is that it should be beautiful first, and then just as blue as may be consistent with its best possible beauty. Moreover, any experienced colourist knows that the blues will be more telling—more purely blue—by the juxtaposition of rightly placed complementary colour. How it may be done is shown in the plan, for, as I cannot have these gardens myself, it will be some consolation to suggest to those who may be in sympathy with my views, how they may be made.

The Grey garden is so called because most of its plants have grey foliage, and all the carpeting and bordering plants are grey or whitish. The flowers are white, lilac, purple and pink. It is a garden mostly for August, because August is the time when the greater number of suitable plants are in bloom; but a Grey garden could also be made for September, or even October, because of the number of Michaelmas Daisies that can be brought into use.

A plan is given of a connected series of gardens of special colouring. For the sake of clearness they are shown in as simple a form as possible, but the same colour scheme could be adapted to others of more important design and larger extent.

The Gold garden is chosen for the middle, partly because it contains the greater number of permanent shrubs and is bright and cheerful all the year round, and partly because it is the best preparation, according to natural colour law, for the enjoyment of the compartments on either side. It is supposed that the house is a little way away to the north, with such a garden scheme close to it as may best suit its style and calibre. Then I would have a plantation of shrubs and trees. The shade and solidity of this would rest and refresh the eye and mind, making them the more ready to enjoy the colour garden. Suddenly entering the Gold garden, even on the dullest day, will be like coming into sunshine. Through the shrub-wood there is also a path to right and left parallel to the long axis of the colour garden, with paths turning south at its two ends, joining the ends of the colour-garden paths. This has been taken into account in arranging the sequence of the compartments.

The hedges that back the borders and form the partitions are for the most part of Yew, grown and clipped to a height of seven feet. But in the case of the Gold garden, where the form is larger and more. free than in the others, there is no definite hedge, but a planting of unclipped larger gold Hollies, and the beautiful golden Plane, so cut back and regulated as to keep within the desired bounds. This absence of a stiff hedge gives more freedom of aspect and a better cohesion with the shrub-wood.

In the case of the Grey garden the hedge is of Tamarisk (*Tamarix gallica*), whose feathery grey-green is in delightful harmony with the other foliage greys. It will be seen on the plan that where this joins the

A SEPTEMBER GREY GARDEN.

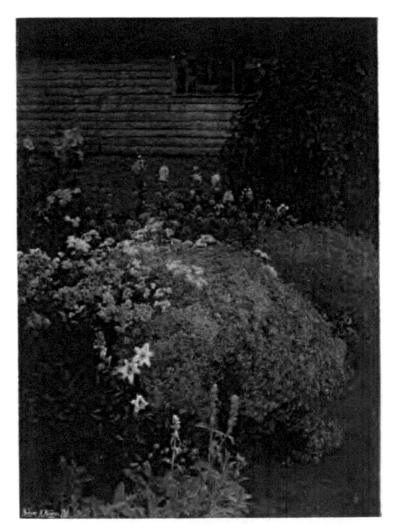

*THE GREY BORDER: PINK HOLLYHOCK, ECHINOPS,
ACHILLEA PEARL, GYPSOPHILA, STACHYS, etc.*

Gold garden the hedge is double, for it must be of gold Holly on one side and of Tamarisk on the other. At the entrances and partition where the path passes, the hedge shrubs are allowed to grow higher, and are eventually trained to form arches over the path.

In the Gold and Green gardens the shrubs, which form the chief part of the planting, are shown as they will be after some years' growth. It is best to have them so from the first. If, in order to fill the space at once, several are planted where one only should eventually stand, the extra ones being removed later, the one left probably does not stand quite right. I strongly counsel the placing of them singly at first, and that until they have grown, the space should be filled with temporary plants. Of these, in the Gold garden, the most useful will be *Œnothera lamarckiana, Verbascum olympicum* and *V. phlomoides*, with more Spanish Broom than the plan shows till the gold Hollies are grown ; and yellow-flowered annuals, such as the several kinds of *Chrysanthemum coronarium*, both single and double, and *Coreopsis Drummondi;* also a larger quantity of African Marigolds, the pale primrose and the lemon-coloured. The fine tall yellow Snapdragons will also be invaluable. Flowers of a deep orange colour, such as the orange African Marigold, so excellent for their own use, are here out of place, only those of pale and middle yellow being suitable.

In such a garden it will be best to have, next the path, either a whole edging of dwarf, gold-variegated Box-bushes about eighteen inches to two feet high, or a mixed planting of these and small bushes of

SPECIAL COLOUR GARDEN—GENERAL PLAN

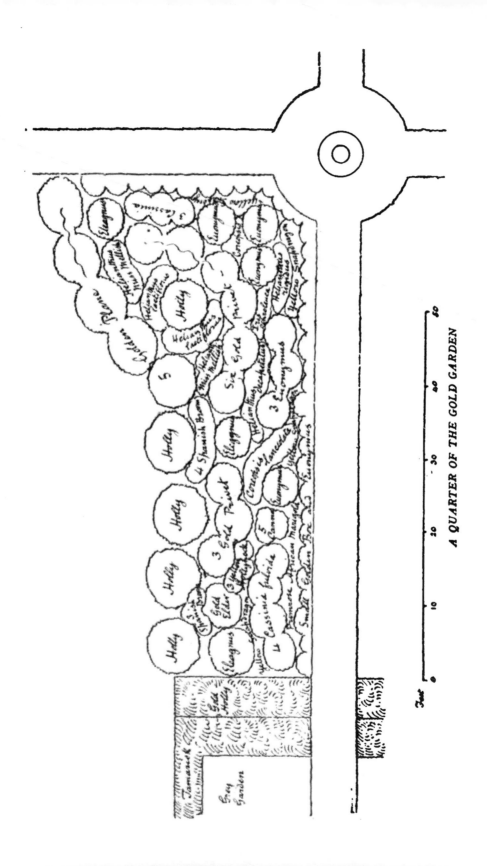

A QUARTER OF THE GOLD GARDEN

THE ORANGE GARDEN

THE GREY GARDEN

THE BLUE GARDEN

FEET 0 10 20 30 40 50

THE GREEN GARDEN

gold-variegated Euonymus clipped down to not much
over two feet. The edge next the path would be
kept trimmed to a line.

The strength of colour and degree of variation are
so great that it is well worth going to a nursery to
pick out all these gold-variegated plants. It is not
enough to tell the gardener to get them. There
should be fervour on the part of the garden's owner
such as will take him on a gold-plant pilgrimage to all
good nurseries within reach, or even to some rather
out of reach. No good gardening comes of not
taking pains. All good gardening is the reward of
well-directed and strongly sustained effort.

Where, in the Gold garden, the paths meet and
swing round in a circle, there may be some accentuating ornament—a sundial, a stone vase for flowers,
or a tank for a yellow Water-lily. If a sundial, and
there should be some incised lettering, do not have
the letters gilt because it is the Gold garden ; the
colour and texture of gilding are quite out of place.
If there is a tank, do not have goldfish ; their colour
is quite wrong. Never hurt the garden for the sake
of the tempting word.

The word " gold " in itself is, of course, an absurdity ;
no growing leaf or flower has the least resemblance
to the colour of gold. But the word may be used
because it has passed into the language with a commonly accepted meaning.

I have always felt a certain hesitation in using the
free-growing perennial Sunflowers. For one thing, the
kinds with the running roots are difficult to keep in

*A DETAIL OF THE GREY SEPTEMBER GARDEN.
PERENNIAL ASTERS AND WHITE CHINA ASTER
MAMMOTH IN FRONT.*

ERYNGIUM AND LILIUM CANDIDUM WITH YUCCAS.

check, and their yearly transplantation among other established perennials is likely to cause disturbance and injury to their neighbours. Then, in so many neglected gardens they have been let run wild, surviving when other plants have been choked, that, half unconsciously, one has come to hold them cheap and unworthy of the best use. I take it that my own impression is not mine alone, for often when I have been desired to do planting-plans for flower borders, I have been asked not to put in any of these Sunflowers, because " they are so common."

But nothing is " common " in the sense of base or unworthy if it is rightly used, and it seems to me that this Gold garden is just the place where these bright autumn flowers may be employed to great advantage. I have therefore shown *Helianthus rigidus* and its tall-growing variety *Miss Mellish*, although the colour of both is quite the deepest I should care to advise ; the paler yellow of *H. lætiflorus* being better, especially the capital pale form of this Sunflower, and of one that I know as a variety of *H. orgyalis*, described at p. 72.

The golden Planes, where the path comes in from the north, are of course deciduous, and it might be well to have gold Hollies again at the back of these, or gold Yews, to help the winter effect.

In some places in the plan the word " gold " has been omitted, but the yellow-leaved or yellow-variegated form of the shrub is always intended. There is a graceful cut-leaved Golden Elder that is desirable, as well as the common one.

Perhaps the Grey garden is seen at its best by reaching it through the orange borders. Here the eye becomes filled and saturated with the strong red and yellow colouring. D on the plan stands for Dahlia; the other plant names are written in full. This filling with the strong, rich colouring has the natural effect of making the eye eagerly desirous for the complementary colour, so that, standing by the inner Yew arch and suddenly turning to look into the Grey garden, the effect is surprisingly—quite astonishingly—luminous and refeshing. One never knew before how vividly bright Ageratum could be, or Lavender or Nepeta; even the grey-purple of Echinops appears to have more positive colour than one's expectation would assign to it. The purple of the Clematises of the Jackmanii class becomes piercingly brilliant, while the grey and glaucous foliage looks strangely cool and clear.

The plan shows the disposition of the plants, with grey-white edging of *Cineraria maritima*, Stachys and Santolina. There are groups of Lavender with large-flowered Clematises (C in the plan) placed so that they may be trained close to them and partly over them. There are the monumental forms of the taller Yuccas, Y. *gloriosa* and its variety *recurva* towards the far angles, and, nearer the front (marked Yucca in plan), the free-blooming *Yucca filamentosa* of smaller size. The flower-colouring is of purple, pink and white. Besides the Yuccas, the other white flowers are *Lilium longiflorum* and *Lilium candidum* (L C on plan), the clear white Achillea The Pearl

YUCCAS AND GREY FOLIAGE.

A FRONT EDGE OF GREY FOLIAGE.

and the grey-white clouds of *Gypsophila paniculata*. The pink flowers are Sutton's Godetia Double Rose, sown in place early in May, the beautiful clear pink Hollyhock Pink Beauty and the pale pink Double Soapwort. Clematis and white Everlasting Pea are planted so that they can be trained to cover the Gypsophila when its bloom is done and the seed-pods are turning brown. As soon as it loses its grey colouring the flowering tops are cut off, and the Pea and Clematis, already brought near, are trained over. When the Gypsophila is making its strong growth in May, the shoots are regulated and supported by some stiff branching spray that is stuck among it. A little later this is quite hidden, but it remains as a firm substructure when the top of the Gypsophila is cut back and the other plants are brought over.

Elymus is the blue-green Lyme-grass, a garden form of the handsome blue-leaved grass that grows on the seaward edges of many of our sea-shore sandhills. The Soapwort next to it is the double form of *Saponaria officinalis*, found wild in many places.

Of Ageratum two kinds are used — a brightly coloured one of the dwarf kinds for places near the front, where it tells as a close mass of colour, and the tall *A. mexicanum* for filling up further back in the border, where it shows as a diffuse purple cloud. The Nepeta is the good garden Catmint (*N. Mussini*). Its normal flowering-time is June, but it is cut half back, removing the first bloom, by the middle of the month, when it at once makes new flowering shoots.

Now, after the grey plants, the Gold garden looks

extremely bright and sunny. A few minutes suffice
to fill the eye with the yellow influence, and then we
pass to the Blue garden, where there is another delightful shock of eye-pleasure. The brilliancy and purity
of colour are almost incredible. Surely no blue
flowers were ever so blue before! That is the impression received. For one thing, all the blue flowers
used, with the exception of Eryngium and *Clematis
davidiana*, are quite pure blues; these two are grey-
blues. There are no purple-blues, such as the bluest
of the Campanulas and the perennial Lupines; they
would not be admissible. With the blues are a few
white and palest yellow flowers; the foam-white
Clematis recta, a delightful foil to Delphinium Belladonna; white perennial Lupine with an almond-like
softness of white; *Spiræa Aruncus*, another foam-
coloured flower. Then milk-white Tree Lupine, in
its carefully decreed place near the bluish foliage of
Rue and Yucca. Then there is the tender citron of
Lupine Somerset and the full canary of the tall yellow
Snapdragon, the diffused pale yellow of the soft plumy
Thalictrum and the strong canary of *Lilium szovitzianum*, with white Everlasting Pea and white Hollyhock
at the back. White-striped Maize grows up to cover
the space left empty by the Delphiniums when their
bloom is over, and pots of *Plumbago capense* are
dropped in to fill empty spaces. One group of this
is trained over the bluish-leaved *Clematis recta*, which
goes out of flower with the third week of July.

Yuccas, both of the large and small kinds, are also
used in the Blue garden, and white Lilies, *candidum*

and *longiflorum*. There is foliage both of glaucous and of bright green colour, besides an occasional patch of the silvery *Eryngium giganteum*. At the front edge are the two best Funkias, *F. grandiflora*, with leaves of bright yellow-green, and *F. Sieboldi*, whose leaves are glaucous. The variegated Coltsfoot is a valuable edge-plant where the yellowish white of its bold parti-colouring is in place, and I find good use for the variegated form of the handsome Grass *Glyceria* or *Poa aquatica*. Though this is a plant whose proper place is in wet ground, it will accommodate itself to the flower border, but it is well to keep it on the side away from the sun. It harmonises well in colour with the Coltsfoot ; as a garden plant it is of the same class as the old Ribbon Grass, but is very much better. It is a good plan to replant it late in spring in order to give it a check ; if this is not done it has a rather worn-out appearance before the end of the summer ; but if it is replanted or divided late in April it stands well throughout the season. The great white-striped Japanese grass, *Eulalia japonica striata* (E U on the plan), is planted behind the Delphiniums at the angles, and groups well with the Maize just in front.

From the Blue garden, passing eastward, we come to the Green garden. Shrubs of bright and deep green colouring and polished leaf-surface predominate. Here are green Aucubas and Skimmias, with *Ruscus racemosus*, the beautiful Alexandrian or Victory Laurel, and more polished foliage of *Acanthus, Funkia, Asarum, Lilium candidum* and *longiflorum*, and *Iris fœtidissima*. Then feathery masses of paler green, Male Fern and

Lady Fern and *Myrrhis odorata*, the handsome fern-like Sweet Cicely of old English gardens.   In the angles are again Eulalias, but these are the variety *zebrina* with the leaves barred across with yellow.

In the Green garden the flowers are fewer and nearly all white—Campanulas *macrantha alba* and *persicifolia*, Lilies, Tulips, Foxgloves, Snapdragons, Peonies, Hellebores—giving just a little bloom for each season to accompany the general scheme of polished and fern-like foliage. A little bloom of palest yellow shows in the front in May and June, with the flowers of Uvularia and Epimedium. But the Green garden, for proper development, should be on a much larger scale.

HARDY GRAPE VINE ON SOUTH SIDE OF HOUSE.

HARDY GRAPE VINE ON HOUSE WALL.

CHAPTER XIII

CLIMBING PLANTS

WHEN one sees climbing plants or any of the shrubs that are so often used as climbers, planted in the usual way on a house or wall, about four feet apart and with no attempt at arrangement, it gives one that feeling of regret for opportunities lost or misused which is the sentiment most often aroused in the mind of the garden critic in the great number of pleasure-grounds that are planted without thought or discernment. Not infrequently in passing along a country road, with eye alert to note the beauties that are so often presented by little wayside cottage gardens, something is seen that may well serve as a lesson in better planting. The lesson is generally one that teaches greater sim-plicity—the doing of one thing at a time ; the avoidance of overmuch detail. One such cottage has under the parlour window an old bush of *Pyrus japonica*. It had been kept well spurred back and must have been a mass of gorgeous bloom in early spring. The rest of the cottage was embowered in an old Grape Vine, perhaps of all wall plants the most beautiful, and, I always think, the most harmonious with cottages or small houses of the cottage class. It would seem to be least in place on the walls of houses of classical type ;

indeed, such houses are often better without any wall-plants. Still, there are occasions where the noble polished foliage of Magnolia comes admirably on their larger spaces, and the clear-cut refinement of Myrtle on their lesser areas of wall-surface.

It is, like all other matters of garden planning, a question of knowledge and good taste. The kind of wall or house and its neighbouring forms are taken into account and a careful choice is made of the most suitable plants. For my own part I like to give a house, whatever its size or style, some dominant note in wall-planting. In my own home, which is a house of the large cottage class, the prevailing wall-growths are Vines and Figs in the south and west, and in a shady northward facing court between two projecting wings, *Clematis montana* on the two cooler sides, and again a Vine upon the other. At one angle on the warmer side of the house, where the height to the eaves is not great, China Roses have been trained up, and Rosemary, which clothes the whole foot of the wall, is here encouraged to rise with them. The colour of the China Rose bloom and the dusky green of the Rosemary are always to me one of the most charming combinations. In remembrance of the cottage example lately quoted there is *Pyrus japonica* under the long sitting-room window. I remember another cottage that had a porch covered with the golden balls of *Kerria japonica*, and China Roses reaching up the greater part of the low walls of half timber and plastering; the pink Roses seeming to ask one which of them were the loveliest in colour; whether it was those that came against the

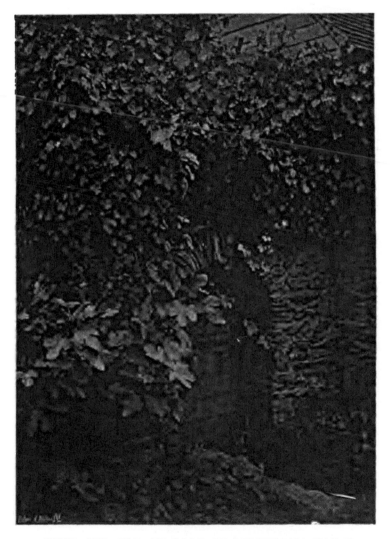

VINE AND FIG AT DOOR OF MUSHROOM HOUSE.

CLEMATIS MONTANA AT ANGLE OF COURT.

CLEMATIS MONTANA OVER WORKSHOP WINDOW.

CLEMATIS MONTANA TRAINED AS GARLANDS.

silver-grey of the old oak or those that rested on the warm-white plaster. It should be remembered that of all Roses the pink China is the one that is more constantly in bloom than any other, for its first flowers are perfected before the end of May, and in sheltered places the later ones last till Christmas.

The *Clematis montana* in the court riots over the wall facing east and up over the edge of the roof. At least it appears to riot, but is really trained and regulated ; the training favouring its natural way of throwing down streamers and garlands of its long bloom-laden cordage. At one point it runs through and over a Guelder Rose that is its only wall companion. Then it turns to the left and is trained in garlands along a moulded oak beam that forms the base of a timbered wall with plastered panels.

But this is only one way of using this lovely climbing plant. Placed at the foot of any ragged tree—old worn-out Apple or branching Thorn—or a rough brake of Bramble and other wild bushes, it will soon fill or cover it with its graceful growth and bounteous bloom. It will rush up a tall Holly or clothe an old hedgerow where thorns have run up and become thin and gappy, or cover any unsightly sheds or any kind of outbuilding. All Clematises prefer a chalky soil, but *montana* does not insist on this, and in my pictures they are growing in sandy ground. In the end of May it comes into bloom, and is at its best in the early days of June. When the flowers are going over and the white petals show that slightly shrivelled surface that comes before they fall, they give off a sweet scent like vanilla. This cannot always be smelt from the actual flowers, but is carried by the air blowing over the flowering mass ; it is a thing that is often a puzzle to owners of gardens some time in the second week of June.

Another of these Clematises, which, like the *montana* of gardens, is very near the wild species and is good for all the same purposes, is *C. Flammula*, blooming in September. Very slightly trained it takes the form of flowery clouds. The illustrations show it used in various ways, on a cottage, on an oak-paled fence and on a wall combined with the feathery foliage of *Spiræa Lindleyana*. I do not think there is any incident in my garden that has been more favourably noticed than the happy growth of these two plants together. The wall faces north a little west, and every year it is a delight to see not only the beauty of associated form, but the loveliness of the colouring ; for the Clematis bloom has the warm white of foam and the Spiræa has leaves of the rather pale green of Lady Fern, besides a graceful fern-like form and a slight twist or turn also of a fern-like character. But this Clematis has many other uses, for bowers, arches and pergolas, as well as for many varied aspects of wild gardening.

A shrub for wall use that is much neglected, though of the highest beauty, is *Abutilon vitifolium*. In our northern and midland counties it may not be hardy, but it does well anywhere south of London. The flowers, each two and a half inches across, are borne in large, loose clusters, their tender lavender colour harmonising perfectly with the greyish, downy foliage.

There is no lovelier or purer blue than that of the

ABUTILON VITIFOLIUM.

CLEMATIS FLAMMULA AND SPIRÆA LINDLEYANA ON A WALL.

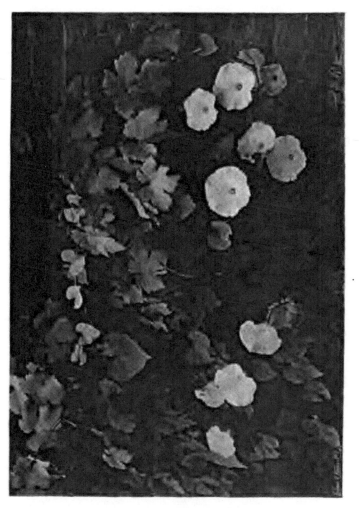

IPOMÆA "HEAVENLY BLUE" AND CHASSELAS VINE.

SOLANUM JASMINOIDES.

CLEMATIS FLAMMULA ON ANGLE OF COTTAGE.

CLEMATIS FLAMMULA ON COTTAGE.

CLEMATIS FLAMMULA ON A WOODEN FENCE.

SWEET VERBENA.

newly opened *Ipomea rubro-cærulea*, popularly known as Heavenly Blue and well deserving the name. It must be raised in heat early in the year and be put out in June against a warm wall. Here it is in a narrow border at the foot of a wall facing south-west, where, by the aid of a few short pea-sticks, it climbs into the lower branches of a Vine. The Vine is one of the Chasselas kind, with leaves of a rather pale green, almost yellowish-green colouring that makes the best possible foil to the pure blue of the Ipomea. To my eye it is the most enjoyable colour-feast of the year. *Solanum crispum*, with purple flowers in goodly bunches, is one of the best of wall shrubs.

Another of the tender plants that is beautiful for walls and for free rambling over other wall-growths is *Solanum jasminoides*. Its white clusters come into bloom in middle summer and persist till latest autumn. In two gardens near me it is of singular beauty ; in the one case on the sunny wall of a sheltered court where it covers a considerable space, in the other against a high south retaining-wall where, from the terrace above, the flowers are seen against the misty woodland of the middle distance and the pure grey-blue of the far-away hills. Turning round on the very same spot, there is the remarkable growth of the Sweet Verbena, that owes its luxuriance to its roots and main shoots being under shelter. There must be unending opportunities, where there are verandahs, of having just such bowers of sweetness to brush against in passing and to waft scented air to the windows of the roo ns above.

These notes can only touch upon the more careful use of a few of the many climbing plants and trailing shrubs. One of the many garden possessions that. I ardently desire and can never have is a bit of rocky hill-side ; a place partly of sheer scarp and partly of tumbled and outcropping rock-mass, for the best use of these plants. There would be the place for the yellow winter Jasmine, for the Honeysuckles both bushy and rambling, for the trailing Clematises lately described and for the native *C. Vitalba*, beautiful both in flower and fruit ; for shrubs like *Forsythia suspensa* and *Desmodium penduliflorum*, that like to root high and then throw down cascades of bloom, and for the wichuraiana Roses, also for Gourds and wild Vines. There should be a good quarter of a mile of it so that one might plant at perfect ease, one thing at a time or one or two in combination, in just such sized and shaped groups as would make the most delightful pictures, and in just the association that would show the best assortment.

I have seen long stretches of bare chalky banks for year after year with nothing done to dispel their bald monotony, feeling inward regret at the wasted opportunity ; thinking how beautiful they might be made with a planting of two common things, *Clematis Vitalba* and Red Spur Valerian. But such examples are without end.

CHAPTER XIV

GROUPINGS OF PLANTS IN POTS

IT is a common thing in Italian gardens to see a quantity of plants in pots standing in various parts of the garden, generally in connection with paved terraces and steps. This is in addition to the larger pot plants —Oranges, Lemons, Oleanders, &c.—that, in their immense and often richly decorated earthenware receptacles, form an important part of the garden design. In our climate we cannot have these unless there is an Orangery or some such spacious place free from frost for housing them in winter. But good groupings of smaller plants in pots is a form of ornament that might be made more use of in our own gardens, especially where there are paved spaces near a house or in connection with a tank or fountain, so that there is convenient access to means of daily watering. I have such a space in a cool court nearly square in shape. A middle circle is paved, and all next the house is paved, on a level of one shallow step higher. It is on the sides of this raised step that the pot plants are grouped, leaving free access to a wooden seat in the middle, and a clear way to a door on the left.

The first thing is to secure good greenery. On each side three oblong Italian terra-cotta pots full of *Funkia*

grandiflora stand on the lower level. They serve to
hide the common flower-pots that are ranged behind.
The picture shows how it looks a day or two after it
is first arranged, early in June when the *Clematis
montana* is still in bloom. Next above the ornamental
pots are common ones, also with *Funkia grandiflora*.
On the inner side of the groups, next the house, are pots
of Aspidistra, and, against the wall, of Male Fern, and
there are more Ferns and Funkias for filling spaces
between the flowering plants. Of these the most
important are Lilies—*longiflorum, candidum* and
speciosum—and Hydrangeas, but we also have pots of
Spanish Irises, of *Gladiolus Colvillei* The Bride, *Campanula persicifolia* and *C. pyramidalis,* of white and
pink Phloxes and of white and pink Cup-and-saucer
Canterbury Bells. The last are taken up from the
ground and potted only just before they come into bloom.

There are seldom more than two kinds of flowering
plants placed here at a time ; the two or three sorts of
beautiful foliage are in themselves delightful to the eye ;
often there is nothing with them but Lilies, and one
hardly desires to have more. There is an ample filling
of the green plants, so that no pots are seen.

If the place were in the sun the plants chosen would
be largely Geraniums ; two-year-old plants in good-
sized pots ; and, in place of the Ferns that enjoy shade
and the Funkias whose leaves often burn in the sun,
there would be the large-leaved *Megasea cordifolia.*
Here also would be Lilies, Hydrangeas and Cannas,
and good store of the graceful Maiden's Wreath
(*Francoa ramosa*).

POT PLANTS JUST PLACED.

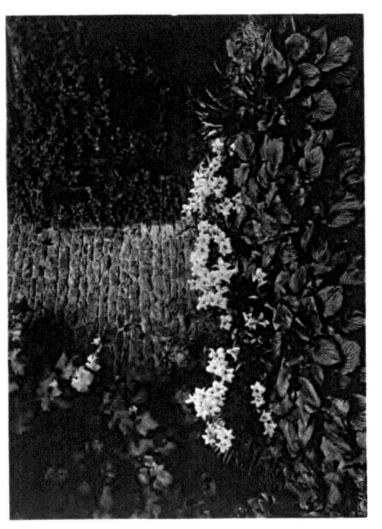

PLANTS IN POTS IN THE SHADED COURT: FUNKIA, LILIUM LONGIFLORUM, FERNS AND ASPIDISTRA.

MAIDEN'S WREATH (FRANCOA RAMOSA).

MAIDEN'S WREATH BY TANK.

The Geraniums would be very carefully assorted for colour ; in one part of the scheme white and soft pink, in another the rosy scarlets, and elsewhere the salmon-reds, now so numerous and good. The last two groups might by degrees tone into the pure scarlets, of which the best I know and the most delightful in colour is Paul Crampel. The colour is pure and brilliant but not *cruel*. I can think of no other word that so well describes some scarlets of a harsh quality that gives discomfort rather than satisfaction to a sensitive colour-eye. Henry Jacoby is to me one of the cruel reds and has no place among my flowers. I have no desire to disparage a plant which is so general a favourite, but feel sure that its popularity is a good deal owing to the fact that the main gardening public is inclined rather to accept what is put before it than to take the trouble to search for something better. Although the colour of this Geranium is extremely vivid, a whole bed of it has a heavy appearance and is wanting in pictorial effect.

I have great pleasure in putting together Omphale, palest salmon-pink ; Mrs. Laurence, a shade deeper ; Mrs. Cannell, a salmon-scarlet approaching the quality of colour of Phlox Coquelicot, and leading these by degrees to the pure, good scarlet of Paul Crampel. A bed or clump or border planted with these, or varieties equivalent in colour, would be seen to have, in comparison with a bed of Henry Jacoby, a quite remarkable degree of life, brilliancy, beauty and interest. The colouring would be actually brighter and yet more kind and acceptable to the eye.

Had I more strength I should visit the nurseries in
order to see all the excellent Geraniums that are now
grown, and to group them into colour-combinations
such as could be confidently recommended. As it is,
I have to depend upon the courtesy of my friends in
the horticultural trade, when I have occasion to make
such combinations, for sending me blooms that I can
choose from.

For detached vases that stand on pedestals, so that
the whole of the vase and contents becomes warmed by
exposure to sunlight, a condition specially grateful to
Geraniums, I know no variety more useful than King
of Denmark. The flowers are in large trusses, half-
double, of an excellent soft salmon-pink colour ; the
foliage is bold and well marked ; the whole plant
massive and handsome. For this and any other out-
door pot-culture it is best if strong two-year-old plants
can be kept.

There are among Geraniums some of a raw magenta-
pink that I regret to see in many gardens and that will
certainly never be admitted into mine.

In designing gardens where there are flagged spaces
it is well to remember the good effect of summer flowers
in slightly raised beds with stone edges. Such beds
often come happily in conjunction with steps and
paved landings and designs in which fountains occur.
Summer flowers, such as Geraniums, Lilies and Cannas,
seem to revel in such beds and are never seen to better
advantage. Owing to the cottage character of my
house I have little scope for such beds—none at all
for the best kind with dwarf walls and curbs of moulded

freestone, but I have one edged with a low wall of local sandstone where there is a square landing paved with the same stone and short flights of steps in connection with a tank and a lower garden level. Here Geraniums and Cannas luxuriate in shelter and full sunshine.

Maiden's Wreath (*Francoa ramosa*) is a plant for many uses. The foliage, though sparing in quantity, is distinct and handsome. The long flower-stems are flung out with a kind of determination of character that would seem to imply that the plant knows what is expected of it and intends to fulfil its settled duty and purpose, namely, that of being a graceful and beautiful ornament. Towards the later summer these flower-stems become so heavy that there is danger of their weight, swayed by a little wind, wrenching out whole portions of the plant. Support should be given with short pieces of hazel stick tied half way up the stem. In nurseries it is general, and even in private gardens not unusual, to see the flowers tied straight upright. This should never be, for it not only forces the plant into a form that is entirely at variance with its nature, but robs it of its natural grace and valuable individuality.

There is no end to the uses of Hydrangeas in pots; a well-bloomed plant will give life and interest to many an uninteresting corner; the bloom is long-enduring and stands equally well in sun and shade. If the blue colour, which comes naturally in some soils, is desired, it can be had by mixing pounded slate and iron filings with the compost—alum is another well-known agent

for inducing the blue colour. But I have much faith
in slate, for the bluest I have ever seen came from a
garden on a slaty soil.

A few only of the many plants that can with advantage be used in pots have been named, but in any
case it would be well to bear in mind that it is best to
restrict the number of kinds shown at once and to make
sure of the good groundwork of foliage.   I have therefore only dwelt upon the few that came to mind as the
best and easiest to use.   But the pretty red and white
single Fuchsias of the Mme. Cornellisson type should
not be forgotten ; and the fine Comet and Ostrich
Plume Asters are capital pot-plants, for, like Canterbury Bells, they bear lifting from the open ground just
before they flower and even in full bloom.

Plants grown in pots lead naturally to the consideration of those most suitable for tubs.   Of these the most
important are permanent things of shrubby nature—
several of the Orange and Lemon family, Oleander,
Pomegranate, Bay, Myrtle, Datura, Sweet Verbena
and dwarf Palm, also Hydrangea, Tree Heliotrope and
Agapanthus.   The last is of course a bulbous plant,
but from its large, solid foliage and quantity of long-
enduring bloom it is one of the best of plants for tubs.
The greater number of these need housing in winter
in an Orangery or other frost-proof building.   Other
bushy plants for tub use that are hardier are some of
the Veronicas, such as *Traversi*, *speciosa* and *hulkeana*,
Olearia Haastii and *O. Gunni*.   Tree Peonies, though
rarely so used, are capital tub plants, and, though they

GERANIUMS AND CANNAS IN A STONE-EDGED BED.

MAIDEN'S WREATH IN POTS ABOVE TANK.

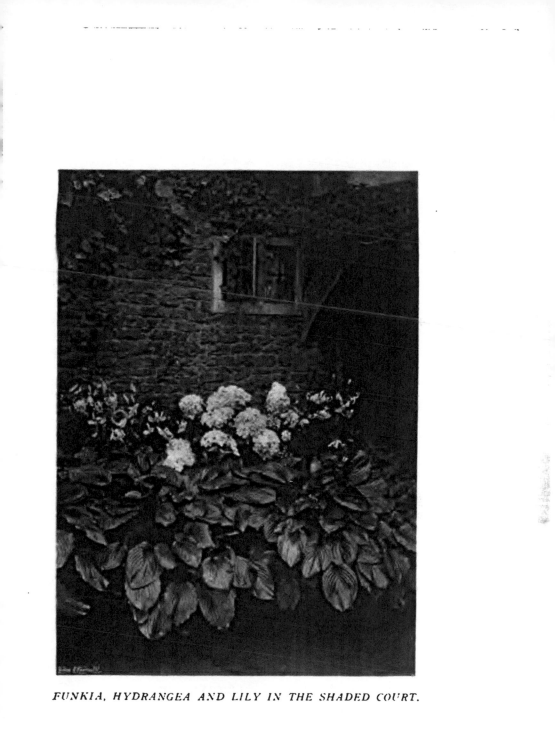

FUNKIA, HYDRANGEA AND LILY IN THE SHADED COURT.

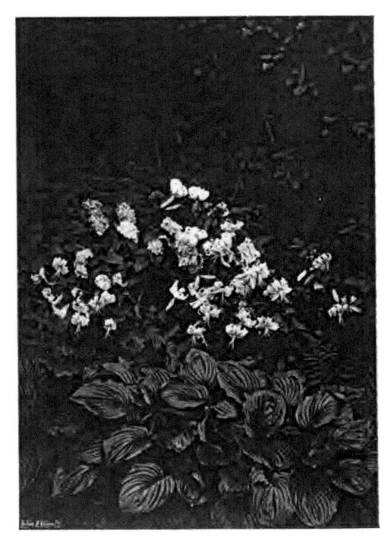

FUNKIA AND LILIUM SPECIOSUM.

are not very long in flower, their supreme beauty makes them desirable. They should certainly be grown in places where labour is not restricted and where there are suitable places for standing such plants away and caring for them in the off season.

For the same kind of use the Tree Lupines, both white and yellow, would be excellent. *Funkia Sieboldi* also makes a handsome tub, while for summer filling Cannas are admirable and old Geraniums in bush form always acceptable. I have never seen Acanthus used in this way, but can see no reason against it. The smaller Bamboos, such as the handsome broad-leaved *B. tessellata*, are very good in tubs. In speaking of plants suitable for tubs, I take the word to include the larger sizes of terra-cotta pots ; but Agapanthus should never be planted in earthenware, as the roots, which remain for many years undisturbed, have so strong a rending power that they will burst anything less resisting than iron-hooped wood.

It is rare to see, anywhere in England, plant-tubs painted a pleasant colour. In nearly every garden they are painted a strong raw green with the hoops black, whereas any green that is not bright and raw would be much better. This matter of the colouring of all such garden accessories as have to be painted deserves more attention than it commonly receives. Doors in garden walls, trellises, wooden railings and hand-gates and seats—all these and any other items of woodwork that stand out in the garden and are seen among its flowers and foliage should, if painted green, be of such a green as does not for brightness come into competition

with the green of leaves.   In the case of tubs especially,
it is the plant that is to be considered first—not the
tub.   The bright, harsh green on the woodwork makes
the colour of the foliage look dull and ineffective.   It
would be desirable, in the case of solitary tub plants,
to study the exact colour that would be most becoming
to the flower and foliage ; but as it is needful, to avoid
a patchy appearance, to paint the whole of the tubs in
any one garden scheme the same colour, a tint should
be chosen that is quiet in itself and that is lower in tone
than the dullest of the foliage in any of the examples·
Moreover, there is no reason for painting the hoops
black ; it is much better to paint the whole out of
one pot.

A good quiet green can be made with black, chrome
No. 1 and white lead, enough white being mixed to
give the depth or lightness desired.   A pretty colour of
paint is much used in France that approximates to the
colourman's malachite green.   This is not the bright
colour of malachite as we know the polished stone,
but a pale, opaque bluish green approaching the tur-
quoise tints.   In the bright, clear climate of France,
and in connection with the higher type of French
architecture, also in more southern countries, the
colour looks very well, though it is not becoming to
some foliage ; but something quieter and more sober
is better suited for England.

Elsewhere I have written of the deplorable effect in
the garden landscape of the glaring white paint—still
worse when tinted blue—that emphasises the ugliness
of the usual greenhouse or conservatory.   This may

LILIUM AURATUM.

A TUB HYDRANGEA.

STEPS AND HYDRANGEAS.

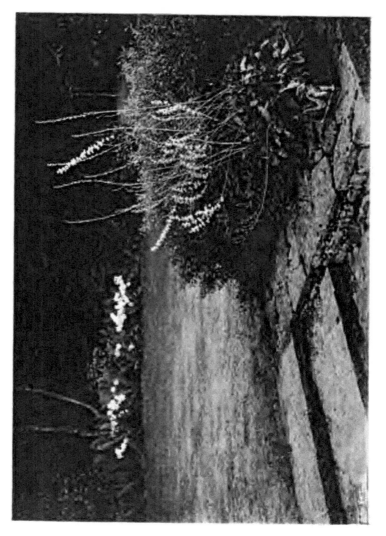

THE NARROW SOUTH LAWN.

be mitigated, if the unsightly structure cannot be concealed, by adding to the white a good deal of black and raw umber, till the paint is of the quiet warm grey that for some strange reason is known to house-painters as Portland-stone colour.

CHAPTER XV

SOME GARDEN PICTURES

WHEN the eye is trained to perceive pictorial effect, it is frequently struck by something—some combination of grouping, lighting and colour—that is seen to have that complete aspect of unity and beauty that to the artist's eye forms a picture. Such are the impressions that the artist-gardener endeavours to produce in every portion of the garden. Many of these good intentions fail, some come fairly well; a few reward him by a success that was beyond anticipation. When this is the case it is probably due to some cause that had been overlooked but that had chanced to complete his intention, such as the position of the sun in relation to some wished-for colour-picture. Then there are some days during the summer when the quality of light seems to tend to an extraordinary beauty of effect. I have never been able to find out how the light on these occasions differs from that of ordinary fine summer days, but, when these days come, I know them and am filled with gladness.

In the case of my own garden, so far as deliberate intention goes, what is aimed at is something quite simple and devoid of complication ; generally one thing or a very limited number of flowering things at a time, but that one, or those few things, carefully placed so as to avoid fuss, and give pleasure to the eye and ease to the mind. In many cases the aim has been to show some delightful colour combination without regard to the other considerations that go to the making of a more ambitious picture. It may be a group in a shrub border, or a combination of border and climbing plants, or some carefully designed company of plants in the rock garden. I have a little rose that I call the Fairy Rose. It came to me from a cottage garden, and I have never seen it elsewhere. It grows about a foot high and has blush-pink flowers with the colour deepening to the centre. In character the flower is somewhere between the lovely Blush Boursault at its best and the little De Meaux. It is an inch and a half across and of beautiful form, especially in the half-opened bud. Wishing to enjoy its beauty to the utmost, and to bring it comfortably within sight, I gave it a shelf in raised rock-work and brought near and under it a clear pale lilac Viola and a good drift of *Achillea umbellata*. It was worth doing. Another combination that gives me much pleasure is that of the pink Pompon Rose Mignonette with Catmint and whitish foliage, such as Stachys or *Artemisia stelleriana*. I may have mentioned this before, but it is so pretty that it deserves repetition.

In a shrubbery border the fine *Spiræa Aruncus* is beautiful with an interplanting of *Thalictrum purpureum*. At the end of a long flower-clump there is a yew hedge coming forward at right angles to the length of the border. Behind the hedge is a stone wall with an arch, through which the path in front of the border passes. Over the stone arch, and rambling partly over the yews, are the vigorous many-flowered growths of *Clematis Flammula.* At the end of the border are pale sulphur-coloured Hollyhocks. Both in form and colour this was a delightful picture ; the foam-like masses of the Clematis resting on the dusky richness of the yew ; the straight shafts of the Holly-hock giving clear colour and agreeing with the upright lines of the sides of the archway, which showed dimly in the shade. These are only a few incidents out of numbers that occur or are intentionally arranged.

There is a place near my house where a path leads down through a nut-walk to the further garden. It is crossed by a shorter path that ends at a Birch-tree with a tall silvered trunk. It seemed desirable to accentuate the point where the paths cross ; I therefore put down four square platforms of stone " pitching " as a place for the standing of four Hydrangeas in tubs. Just before the tree is a solid wooden seat and a shallow wide step done with the same stone pitching. Tree and seat are surrounded on three sides by a rectangular planting of yews. The tender greys of the rugged lower bark of the Birch and the silvering of its upper stem tell finely against the dark velvet-like richness of the Yew and the leaf-mass of other trees beyond ; the pink flowers and fresh green foliage of the Hydran-geas are also brilliant against the dusky green. It is just one simple picture that makes one glad for three months of the later summer and early autumn. The longer cross-path, which on the right leads in a few

HYDRANGEA TUBS AND BIRCH-TREE SEAT.

HYDRANGEA TUBS AND NUT WALK.

yards to steps up to the paved court on the north side of the house, on the left passes down the nut-walk, as the second illustration shows. The Birch-tree and seat are immediately to the right, just out of the picture. Standing a little way down the shaded nut-walk and looking back, the Hydrangeas are seen in another aspect, with the steps and house behind them in shade, and the sun shining through their pale green leaves. Sitting on the seat, the eye, passing between the pink Hydrangea flowers, sees a short straight path bounded by a wall of Tree Box to right and left, and at the far end one tub of pale blue Hydrangea in shade, backed by a repetition of the screen of Yews such as enclose the Birch-tree.

On the south side of the house there is a narrow border full of Rosemary, with China Roses and a Vine, as shown in the illustration opposite p. 114. Here the narrow lawn, backed by woodland, is higher than the house-level. Shallow steps lead up to it in the middle, and to right and left is low dry-walling. On the upper edge of this is a hedge of Scotch Briars, shown in full bloom at p. 50, and in the narrow border below, a planting of the low-growing *Andromeda* (*Leucothoë*) *axillaris*, a little shrub that is neat throughout the year and in winter prettily red-tinted.

The beautiful White Lily cannot be grown in the hot sandy soil of my garden. Even if its place be ever so well prepared with the loam and lime that it loves, the surrounding soil-influences seem to rob it of its needful nourishment; it makes a miserable show for one year and never appears again. The only way to grow it is in pots or tubs sunk in the soil. For some years I had wished to have an orderly planting of this lovely Lily in the lower border at the back of the Andromeda just in front of the Briars. I had no flower-pots deep enough, or wide enough at the bottom, but was able to make a contrivance with some short, broad, unglazed drain-pipes, measuring a foot long and of about the same diameter, by cementing in an artificial bottom made of pieces of roofing-tile and broken flower-pot, leaving spaces for drainage. Then three bulbs were put in each pot in a compost that I knew they would enjoy. When they were half grown the pots were sunk in holes at nearly even distances among the Andromedas, and in a few weeks my row of Lilies gave me my reward. Other Lilies (*L. longiflorum*) follow them a month later, just beyond in the wood edge among tufts of Male Fern, and a pot of Francoa is to right and left of the shallow steps.

During the last year or two some pretty incidents have occurred about these same steps ; not important enough to call garden pictures, but charming and interesting and easily enjoyable because they are close to the open garden door of the sitting-room and because they teach me to look out for the desirable things that come of themselves. A seedling of the wild Clematis (*C. Vitalba*) appeared among the Briars to the left. As it was too strong a plant to let grow over them unchecked, I pulled it forward towards the steps, training one or two shoots to run along the hollow of the step and laying on them pieces of stone, invisible among the foliage, to keep them from being dislodged

WHITE LILIES.

THE STEPS AND THEIR INCIDENTS.

by the skirts of visitors or the gambols of my cats
At the same time, in a crack of the stone just below
the upper step there came a seedling of the tall Chimney
Campanula (*C. pyramidalis*). The second year this
threw up its tall flower-stem and was well in bloom
when it was wrecked by an early autumn gale, the
wind wrenching out the crown and upper root-stock.
But a little shred of rooted life remained, and now there
is again the sturdy tuft promising more flower-stems
for the coming season.

Close behind the Bell-flower a spreading sheet of
Wild Thyme has crept out of the turf and flowed rather
widely over the stone.   Luckily I just saved it from
the tidying process that threatened it, and as it is now
well established over the stone I still have the pleasure
of its bright rosy bloom when the duties of the mowing-
machine rob me of the other tiny flowers—Hawkweed,
Milkwort and Bedstraw—that bloom so bravely in
the intervals between its ruthless but indispensable
ministrations.

CHAPTER XVI

A BEAUTIFUL FRUIT GARDEN

THERE is a whole range of possible beautiful treatment in fruit-growing that is rarely carried out or even attempted. Hitherto but little has been done to make the fruit garden a place of beauty ; we find it almost flaunting its unloveliness, its white painted orchard-houses and vineries, its wires and wire-nettings. It is not to be denied that all these are necessary, and that the usual and most obvious way of working them does not make for beauty. But in designing new gardens or remodelling old, on a rather large scale, there need be no difficulty in so arranging that all that is necessarily unbeautiful should be kept in one department, so hedged or walled around as to be out of sight.

In addition to such a fruit garden for strict utility I have in mind a walled enclosure of about an acre and a half, longer than wide, laid out as shown in the plan. I have seen in large places just such spaces, actually walled but put to no use.

The wall has trained fruit-trees—Peaches spreading their goodly fans, Pears showing long, level lines, and, including hardy Grape Vines, giving all the best exposition of the hardy fruit-grower's art. Next to the wall is a space six feet wide for ample access to the fruit-trees, their pruning, training and root-management ; then a fourteen-foot plant border, wholly for beauty, and a path eight feet wide. At a middle point on all four sides the high wall has an arched doorway corresponding to the grassy way between the fruit-trees in the middle space. If the wall has some symmetrical building on the outside of each angle, so much the better ; the garden can make use of all. One may be a bothy, with lower extension out of sight ; one a half-underground fruit-store, with bulb-store above ; a third a paint-shop, and a fourth a tea-house.

The middle space is all turf ; in the centre a Mulberry, and, both ways across, double lines of fruit-trees, ending with Bays ; the Bays are at the ends on the plan. In almost any part of the sea-warmed south of England, below the fifty-first parallel of latitude, which passes through the upper part of Sussex, the rows of fruit-trees on the green might be standard Figs ; elsewhere they would be bush Pears and Apples. If the soil is calcareous, so much the better for the Figs and Mulberry, the Vines and indeed nearly all the fruits. The angle-clumps in the grass are planted with Magnolias, Yuccas and Hydrangeas.

The border all round is for small shrubs and plants of some solidity or importance ; the spaces are too long for an ordinary flower border. It would have a good bush of *Magnolia stellata* at each angle, Yuccas, Tritomas, hardy Fuchsias, Peonies, *Euphorbia Wulfenii*, Hollyhocks, Dahlias, Hydrangeas, Michaelmas Daisies, Flag Iris, the beautiful *Olearia Gunni* and

THE BEAUTIFUL FRUIT GARDEN

O. Haastii, Tree Lupines, Forsythia, Weigela, the smaller Bush Spiræas, Veronicas, Tamarisk, the large-bloomed Clematises, bush kinds of garden Roses, Funkias, and so on.

Surely my fruit garden would be not only a place of beauty, of pleasant sight and pleasant thought, but of leisurely repose, a repose broken only faintly and in welcome fashion by its own interests—in July, August and September a goodly place in which to wander and find luscious fruits in quantity that can be gathered and eaten straight from the tree. There is a pleasure in searching for and eating fruit in this way that is far better than having it picked by the gardener and brought in and set before one on a dish in a tame room. Is this feeling an echo of far-away days of savagery when men hunted for their food and rejoiced to find it, or is it rather the poet's delight of having direct intercourse with the good gift of the growing thing and seeing and feeling through all the senses how good and gracious the thing is ? To pass the hand among the leaves of the Fig-tree, noting that they are a little harsh upon the upper surface and yet soft beneath ; to be aware of their faint, dusky scent ; to see the cracking of the coat of the fruit and the yellowing of the neck where it joins the branch—the two indications of ripeness—sometimes made clearer by the drop of honeyed moisture at the eye ; then the handling of the fruit itself, which must needs be gentle because the tender coat is so readily bruised and torn ; at the same time observing the slight greyish bloom and the colouring—low-toned transitions of purple and green ; and finally to have the enjoyment of the luscious pulp, with the knowledge that it is one of the most wholesome and sustaining of fruit foods—surely all this is worthy garden service !   Then how delicious are the sun-warmed Apricots and Peaches, and, later in the year, the Jargonelle Pears, always best eaten straight from the tree ; and the ripe Mulberries of September. And how pleasant to stroll about the wide grassy ways, turning from the fruits to the flowers in the clumps and borders ; to the splendid Yuccas and the masses of Hydrangea bloom, and then to the gorgeous Tritomas and other delights ; and to see the dignity of the stately Bay-trees and the incomparable beauty of their every twig and leaf.

The beautiful fruit garden would naturally lead to the orchard, a place that is not so often included in the pleasure-ground as it deserves. For what is more lovely than the bloom of orchard trees in April and May, with the grass below in its strong, young growth ; in itself a garden of Cowslips and Daffodils. In an old orchard how pictorial are the lines of the low-leaning old Apple-trunks and the swing and poise of their upper branches, best seen in winter when their graceful movement of line and wonderful sense of balance can be fully appreciated. But the younger orchard has its beauty too, of fresh, young life and wealth of bloom and bounteous bearing.

Then if the place of the orchard suggests a return to nearer pleasure-ground with yet some space between, how good to make this into a free garden orchard for the fruits of wilder character ; for wide-spreading

Medlars, for Quinces, again some of the most graceful of small British trees ; for Service, Damson, Bullace, Crabs and their many allies, not fruit-bearing trees except from the birds' and botanists' points of view, but beautiful both in bloom and berry, such as the Mountain Ash, Wild Cherry, Blackthorn, and the large-berried White-thorns, Bird-Cherry, White Beam, Holly and Amelanchier.   Then all these might be inter-grouped with great brakes of the free-growing Roses and the wilder kinds of Clematis and Honeysuckle. And right through it should be a shady path of Filberts or Cobnuts arching overhead and yielding a grateful summer shade and a bountiful autumn harvest.

CHAPTER XVII

PLANTING FOR WINTER COLOUR

MUCH cheerful positive colour, other than that given
by flowers or leaves, may be obtained in winter by
using a good selection of small trees with coloured
bark. Of these the most useful are the Red Dogwood
and some of the Willows. This planting for colour of
bright-barked trees is no new thing, for a good half
century ago the late Lord Somers, at Eastnor Castle
near Malvern, used to " paint his woods," as he
described it, in this way.

The Cardinal Willow has bright red bark, *Salix
britzensis* orange, and the Golden Osier bright yellow.
The yearly growth has the best-coloured bark, so that
when they are employed for giving colour it is usual
to cut them every winter ; moreover, the large quantity of young shoots that the cutting induces naturally
increases the density of the colour effect. But if they
are planted in a rather large way it is better that the
regular winter cutting should be restricted to those
near the outer edge, and to let a good proportion of
those within stand for two or more years, and to
have some in the background that are never cut at
all, but that are allowed to grow to their full size and
to show their natural habit.

It will also be well, instead of planting them exclusively sort by sort, to group and intergroup carefully assorted colours, such as the scarlet Willow with the purple-barked kind, and to let this pass into the American Willow with the black stem. Such a group should not be too large, and it should be near the pathway, for it will show best near at hand. For the sake of the bark-colouring, it would be best to cut it all every year, although in the larger plantings it is desirable to have the trees of different ages, or the effect may be too much that of a mere crop instead of a well-arranged garden grouping.

Some of the garden Roses, both of the free-growing and bush kinds, have finely coloured bark that can be used in much the same way. They are specially good in broken ground, such as the banks of an old hollow cart-way converted to garden use, or the sloping *débris* of a quarry. Of the free kinds, the best coloured are *Rosa ferruginea*, whose leaves are red as well as the stem—it is the *Rosa rubrifolia* of nurseries—and the varieties of Boursault Roses, derived from *Rosa alpina*. As bushes for giving reddish colouring, *Rosa lucida* would be among the best.

By waterside the Great Reedmace—commonly but wrongly called Bulrush—holds its handsome seed-heads nearly through the winter, and beds of the Common Reed (*Arundo Phragmites*) stand up the winter through in masses of light, warm colouring that are grateful to the eye and suggest comfortable harbourage for wildfowl.

Some shrubs have conspicuously green bark, such

as the Spindle-tree ; but the habit of growth is rather too diffuse to let it make a distinct show of colour. *Leycesteria formosa* is being tried in mass for winter colour in some gardens, but I venture to feel a little doubtful of its success ; for though the skin of the half-woody stem is bright green, the plant has the habit of retaining some of its leaves and the remains of its flowering tips till January, or even later. After frost these have the appearance of untidy grey rags, and are distinctly unsightly. The brightest effect of all green-barked plants is that given by Whortleberry, a plant that on peaty or sandy soils is one of the most enjoyable of winter undershrubs.

It would add greatly to the enjoyment of many country places if some portions were planted with evergreens expressly for winter effect. Some region on the outskirts of the garden, and between it and woodland, would be the most desirable. If well done the sense of wintry discomfort would disappear, for nearly all the growing things would be at their best, and even in summer, shrubs and plants can do no more than this. In summer, too, it would be good to see, for the green things would have such an inter-planting of free Roses, Jasmines, Clematis, Honey-suckles, Forsythia, and so on, as would make charming incidents of flower-beauty.

The place for this winter walk should be sheltered from the north and east. I have such a place in my mind's eye, where, beyond the home garden and partly wooded old shrubbery, there is a valley running up into a fir-wooded hill. The path goes up the hill-side diagonally, with a very gentle gradient. In the cooler, lower portion there would be Rhododendrons and Kalmias, with lesser growths of Skimmia and Gaultheria. Close to the path, on the less sunny side, would be Lent Hellebores and the delightful winter greenery of Epimedium. Then in full sun *Andromeda japonica*, and on the shadier side *Andromeda floribunda*. Both of these hard and rather brittle-wooded shrubs belong to the group properly named *Pieris*, and form dense bushes four or more feet high. At their foot would be the lower-growing Andromedas of the *Leucothoë* section, with lissome branches of a more willow-like character. These make a handsome ground-carpeting from one to three feet high, beautiful at all seasons—the leaves in winter tinted or marbled with red. Portions of the cooler side would also have fringes of Hartstongue and Polypody, both winter ferns. Then, as the path rose into more direct sunlight, there would be Cistuses—in all mild winter days giving off their strong, cordial scent—and the dwarf Rhododendrons. Behind the Cistuses would be White Broom, finely green-stemmed in winter. There would even be shrubs in flower ; the thick-set yellowish bloom of Witch Hazel (*Hamamelis*) and the bright yellow of *Jasminum nudiflorum*. Then groups of Junipers, and all the ground carpeted with Heath, and so to the upper Fir-wood. Then, after the comforting greenery of the lower region, the lovely colour of distant winter landscape would be intensely enjoyable ; for the greys and purples of the leafless woodland of middle distance have a beauty that no summer

K

landscape can show. In clear weather the further distances have tints of an extraordinary purity, while the more frequent days of slightly distant haze have another kind of beautiful mystery.

The common Laurel is generally seen as a long-suffering garden hack, put to all sorts of rather ignoble uses. It is so cheap to buy, so quick of growth and so useful as an easily made screen that its better use is, except in rare instances, lost sight of. Planted in thin woodland and never pruned, it grows into a small tree that takes curious ways and shapes of trunk and branch of a character that is remarkably pictorial.

CHAPTER XVIII

FORM IN PLANTING

IF in the foregoing chapters I have dwelt rather insistently on matters of colour, it is not that I underrate the equal importance of form and proportion, but that I think that the question of colour, as regards its more careful use, is either more commonly neglected or has had fewer exponents. As in all matters relating to design in gardening, the good placing of plants in detail is a matter of knowledge of an artistic character. The shaping of every group of plants, to have the best effect, should not only be definitely intended, but should be done with an absolute conviction by the hand that feels the *drawing* that the group must have in relation to what is near, or to the whole form of the clump or border or whatever the nature of the place may be. I am only too well aware that to many this statement may convey no idea whatever; nevertheless I venture to insist upon its truth. Moreover, I am addressing this book to the consideration of those who are in sympathy with my views of gardening, among whom I know there are many who, even if they have not made themselves able, by study and long practice, to show in groundwork and garden design the quality known to artists as *drawing*—by which is

A WILD HEATH GARDEN
Upper Figure: As First Planted.
Lower Figure: After Alteration.

meant a right movement of line and form and group—can at least recognise its value—indeed, its supreme importance—when it is present, and do not, in its absence, fail to feel that the thing shown is without life, spirit, or reasonable justification.

Even a proficiency in some branch of fine art does not necessarily imply ability to lay out ground. I have known, in the intimate association of half a lifetime, a landscape painter whose interpretation of natural beauty was of the most refined and poetical quality, and who truly loved flowers and beautiful vegetation, but who was quite incapable of personally arranging a garden ; although it is more usual that an artist should almost unconsciously place plants well.

It is therefore not to be expected that it is enough to buy good plants and merely to tell the gardener of average ability to plant them in groups, as is now often done with the very best intention. It is impossible for the gardener to know what is meant. In all the cases that have come under my notice, where such indefinite instruction has been given, the things have been planted in stiff blocks. Quite lately I came upon such an example in the garden of a friend who is by no means without a sense of beauty. There was a bank-like space on the outskirts of the pleasure-ground where it was wished to have a wild Heath garden. A better place could hardly be, for the soil is light and sandy and the space lies out in full sunlight. The ground had been thrown about into ridges and valleys, but without any reference to its natural form, whereas with half the labour it might have been guided into slight hollows, ridges and promontories of good line and proportion. I found it planted as in the upper plan; the path stiffly edged with one kind of Heath on one side and another kind on the other; the back planting in rectangular blocks; near the front, bushes of Veronica at exactly even distances, and between each bush the same number of Heaths in every interval quite stiffly planted. Some of the blocks at the back were of Violets—plants quite unsuited to the place. Yet, only leaving out the Violets, all the same plants might have been disposed so as to come quite easily and naturally as shown on the lower plan. Then a thin sowing of the finer Heath grasses, to include the pathway, where alone they would be mown, and a clever interplanting of wild Thyme and the native Wood Sage (*Teucrium Scorodonia*), common on the neighbouring heaths, would have put the whole thing together and would have given the impression, so desirable in wild planting, of the thing having so happened, rather than of its having been artificially made.

In planting or thinning trees also, the whole ultimate good of the effect will depend on this sense of form and good grouping. If these qualities are secured, the result in after years will be a poem; if they are neglected, it will be nothing but a crop.

I can imagine nothing more interesting than the guiding and part-planting of large stretches of natural young woodland, with some hilly ground above and water at the foot. As it is, I have to be content with my little wood of ten acres; yet I am truly glad to have even that small space to treat with reverent thankfulness and watchful care.

INDEX

INDEX

A

ABUTILON vitifolium, 50, 69, 118

Acanthus, 27, 28, 97, 113 ; as tub plant, 127

Achillea umbellata, 50, 131 ; A. Eupatorium, 62, 72 ; The Pearl, 75, 110

Adonis, 27

Æsculus, 76

Agapanthus, 127

Agathea cœlestis, 62, 66, 69

Ageratum, 53, 60, 74, 90, 110, 111

Alexandrian Laurel, 113

Alpenrose, 8, 20, 94

Alyssum, 28

Amelanchier, 13

Anchusa, 46, 49

Andromeda, 8, 15, 20, 35, 94, 133, 145

Anemone sylvestris, 39 ; japonica, 90

Annuals, half hardy, 53, 60 ; hardy, 60

Antennaria, 29

Apples, 137

Arabis, double, 26, 27, 29, 32

Arbutus, 95

Arenaria balearica, 35; montana, 36

Artemisia stelleriana, 66, 75, 89, 131

Arundo Phragmites, 143

Asarum, 18, 36, 113

Aspidistra, 122

Asters, China, 60, 76, 89, 126; perennial, 75, 90, 97

Aubrietia, 26, 29, 32

Aucuba, 113

August, Flower-border in, 68

Azalea, 19, 93

B

BAMBUSA tessellata, 97; as tub plant, 127

Bay, 53, 137

Bedding plants, 53, 80

Begonias, 90; with Megasea, 91

Berberis, 31

Bergamot, 62

Blue flowers, 66, 70

Blue garden, 98, 111

Bracken, 14, 15

Briars, Scotch, 49, 133

Broom, white, 38, 39, 40, 95, 145

Bulb-border, 5

Printed in Great Britain by Butler & Tanner Frome and London,

CPSIA information can be obtained at www.ICGtesting.com
Printed in the USA
241547LV00004B/38/P